THE PROMISE OF THE SPIRIT

Books by
WILLIAM BARCLAY
Published by The Westminster Press

THE PROMISE OF THE SPIRIT

TRAIN UP A CHILD
Educational Ideals in the Ancient World

DAILY STUDY BIBLE

The
PROMISE
of the
SPIRIT

by
WILLIAM BARCLAY

Philadelphia
THE WESTMINSTER PRESS

To the Memory of
A. J. G.
A Man of the Spirit

Contents

Foreword

I SHOULD BE sadly lacking courtesy, if at the beginning of this book I did not express my most sincere thanks to the Publishers for giving to me the privilege of writing it. That is an honour which I much appreciate, and a responsibility of which I have been continually conscious.

No special subject was suggested or laid down. The subject that I have chosen, or rather, the subject which has chosen me, is the teaching of the New Testament about the Holy Spirit. This is a subject of which I had long wished to make a study, and the task of writing this book gave me the opportunity to do so.

I cannot say that I have in this book included every passage in the New Testament which deals with the Holy Spirit, but I can say that I have included more than ninety per cent of such passages. I would wish to say that on this occasion I have deliberately disregarded critical questions of authorship and date and the like, and I have tried simply to take the New Testament passages on the Spirit as they stand. The only place in which any critical matter enters into the subject at all I have passed over in silence. That place is the Pastoral Epistles, and I have included them with the post-Pauline material rather than with the letters of Paul. It has been my purpose simply to take the passages which deal with the Holy Spirit and to try to find, and then to appropriate, their meaning.

I can only say that the study of the teaching of the New Testament about the Holy Spirit has been for me personally a humiliating, a challenging, and a comforting experience— humiliating, because it has been driven home upon me how far short I have come of experiencing the splendour of life in the Spirit; challenging, because I have dimly glimpsed heights of Christian experience which may yet be reached; comforting, because I never before realized the reservoir of divine power which is available for the man who will commit his life to Jesus Christ.

It is my prayer that those who read this book will by their own study come more and more to know the Holy Spirit, not as a doctrine, but as a Person, and that they will thereby experience more of His power in their own lives.

WILLIAM BARCLAY

TRINITY COLLEGE
GLASGOW
August 1959

CHAPTER ONE

Men of the Spirit

IN THE memoir of the author which forms the introduction to Adam C. Welch's book *Kings and Prophets of Israel*, Dr George S. Gunn tells of a text on which Adam Welch loved to preach, and on which he constantly urged his students to preach. The text was: 'Be not drunk with wine, wherein is excess; but be filled with the Spirit' (Ephesians 5[18]). Welch had a gift for the startling and arresting phrase, and he always began his sermon on that text with the blunt announcement: 'You've got to fill a man with something.' It may well be said that the story of the Bible is the story of Spirit-filled men.

And yet for the most part it remains true that our thinking about the Spirit is vaguer and more undefined than our thinking about any other part of the Christian Faith. It is easy to think definitely about God; the very word 'Father' gives us a clear picture of the mind and the heart of God. It is still easier to 'put a face on' Jesus the Son, for we have the vivid pictures of the Gospels to make Jesus come alive before our eyes. But when we think of the Holy Spirit our thoughts are usually much more vague and nebulous and impersonal.

It often happens in life—indeed it happens daily—that we use a thing and benefit from a thing without being fully able to understand all about it. We use electricity without being able to define what electricity is or how it works. We use a motor car without being able to understand the theory of the working of the internal combustion engine. There is many a thing in this life which we know by its effects. For many of us that will be true also of the Holy Spirit. We need not get lost in the mysteries of the Trinity to experience the power of the Holy Spirit; and it will be to the good of our souls to go to the Bible and to meditate on what the Bible says about the work of the Spirit of God in the lives of men, in order that we may lay hold on that power for our own lives. 'I would have him know a little history,' said Oliver Cromwell, when he was arranging for the education of his son Richard. If we can see the working of the Spirit of God in the history of the people of God, and in the lives of the men of God, then we shall know more clearly for what we are asking, when we pray to God to send His Holy Spirit upon us, and to grant us His Spirit.

In his commentary on the *Wisdom of Solomon*, J. A. F. Gregg lays it down that 'for the Old Testament writers the Spirit of God denotes God in His activity in the world'. That is simply to say that there can be no such thing as religion without the Spirit, and that, wherever the Spirit is, there true religion is. That is why we do not need to wait until the days of the New Testament to see the working of the Spirit of God. That Spirit is there powerful and present in the Old Testament also. It is true that we have to wait until the coming of Jesus Christ, and until His Resurrection and His Ascension, before we enter into the full splendour of the work of the Spirit, but it is also true that God never left His world without His Spirit. So, then, let us begin in the Old Testament before we turn to the New Testament.

(1) We meet the Spirit of God in the first words of the Bible, and in its opening sentences. 'The Spirit of God moved upon the face of the waters' (Genesis 1^2). *The Spirit is the agent of God in creation.* Here is something on which the Old Testament lingers more than once. Elihu says to Job: 'The Spirit of God hath made me, and the breath of the Almighty hath given me life' (Job 33^4). The Psalmist has it: 'Thou sendest forth thy Spirit, they are created' (Psalm 104^{30}). It is the Spirit of God who brings existence out of nothingness, order out of chaos, beauty out of blank formlessness. All the thinkers of the ancient times were impressed with the mystery of the dependableness of this world. What is it that ceaselessly maintains the rhythm of night and day, of spring, summer, autumn and winter, of the ebb and flow of the tides, and the rising and the setting of the sun? What is it that maintains the

order of the heavens, in which the heavenly bodies abide unalterably in their own paths? What is it that makes cause and effect predictable, that so orders things that the composition of elements in the same proportion will always produce the same result? What is it that makes this a reliable universe in which we can have faith? What is it that puts the order into things, beyond the change and flux of time? The answer of the Old Testament thinker would be that the Spirit of God brought order into chaos, and maintains the order of the world. The tablet of Sir Christopher Wren in St Paul's Cathedral, which was the creation of the great architect's mind, has the inscription: 'If you would seek his monument, look around you.' If we wish to see the work of the Spirit, we have no further to look than at the wonderful world in which we live, for that world is ordered by the Spirit of God.

But the Old Testament would go further than that, for it tells us that the Spirit is not only God's agent in creation; *the Spirit is also God's agent in re-creation.* History, it has been pessimistically said, is the record of the sins, the follies and the mistakes of men. Certainly it is true that God made all things good, and into the beauty there came the ugliness which is the product of the sin of man. The re-creating and the restoring power is the power of the Spirit. 'The palace will be forsaken, the populous city deserted; the hill and the watchtower will become dens for ever, a joy of wild asses, a pasture of flocks; until the Spirit is poured upon us from on high' (Isaiah 32[14, 15] RSV). The power of the Spirit brought order into the primal chaos, and it is still the power of the Spirit which can restore order to the chaos which the sin and disobedience of men have caused.

The Spirit is God's creating and God's re-creating power both in the world and in the individual life. It was the promise of God to Saul: 'The Spirit of the Lord will come upon thee, and thou shalt prophecy with them, *and shalt be turned into another man*' (1 Samuel 10[6]). Every man needs to be made new; and he can be made new if he opens himself to the recreating power of the Spirit of God.

(2) Great as is the power of the Spirit in creation in the Old Testament, still greater is the power of the Spirit in the lives of individual men. *The great leaders of the Old Testament are men who possess the Spirit, who have been possessed by the Spirit, and in whom the Spirit dwells.*

When Pharaoh decides to entrust the administration of his realm to Joseph, his question is: 'Can we find such a one as this, a man in whom the Spirit of God is?' (Genesis 41³⁸). When the seventy elders are chosen to be the henchmen of Moses in his great task, they are to be fitted for office by the putting of the Spirit upon them (Numbers 11¹⁶⁻¹⁷). Joshua is singled out as the successor of Moses because he is a man in whom the Spirit is (Numbers 27¹⁸). It may be that Judges is one of the most primitive books in the Old Testament, full of stories of battle and bloodshed which are far from the Gospel of love; and yet the strange fact remains that *Men of the Spirit* might well be an alternative title for that book. When Israel needed a deliverer from the power of Mesopotamia, Othniel arose, and the Spirit of the Lord came upon him (Judges 3¹⁰). When the Midianites were terrorizing Israel, the Spirit of the Lord came upon Gideon (Judges 6³⁴). When the Ammonites threatened, the Spirit of the Lord came upon Jephthah (Judges 11²⁹). At the time of the threat of Nahash the Ammonite, the Spirit of the Lord came upon Saul (1 Samuel 11⁶). When David was anointed by Samuel, the Spirit of the Lord came upon him from that day forward (1 Samuel 16¹³). The only true leader of a nation is a man of the Spirit. When God has some great task to give a man, He gives it to a man whose equipment for the task is the presence and the power of the Spirit.

Again the Old Testament goes further than this. All the great heroes whose names we have cited were men of victory; it was through the Spirit that they were raised up, and it was in the Spirit that they triumphed. But in the later part of the Old Testament, in the visions of Isaiah, there arises one whose destiny is to suffer, the Suffering Servant, who, not by his victories, but by his acceptance of bitter suffering, is to be the

saviour of the people of God. And God's word concerning
that greatest of all figures is: 'I have put my Spirit upon him'
(Isaiah 42^1).

The conviction of the Old Testament is that no man can do
the work of God without the Spirit of God, that no man can
lead his fellow-men unless he himself is led by the Spirit of
God. There is no greater problem today in every sphere of
life than the problem of leadership. That problem cannot be
solved apart from the Spirit of God. It is told of D. L.
Moody that in his early days the thought came to him: 'What
could God not do with a man, if a man would submit himself
wholly and entirely to the Spirit of God?' Then there came
the challenge to him: 'Why should I not be that man?' And
history knows what the Spirit of God did with D. L. Moody.
The man who is dedicated to leadership must first be dedicated
to the Spirit of God. The clamant need of both Church
and State is for men who are men of the Spirit, for without the Spirit no amount of intellectual power, no amount
of administrative ability, not even the capacity to toil, will
suffice.

(3) In the Old Testament *the Spirit of God is specially
connected with the gift and the obligation of prophecy.* It is the
Spirit who makes a man a prophet and who gives a man his
message.

It was the Spirit who gave Balaam his message about the
future greatness of Israel (Numbers 24^2). The Spirit of the
Lord came upon Saul, and he prophesied among the prophets
(1 Samuel 10^{10}). 'The Spirit of the Lord spake by me, and
His word was in my tongue', said David (2 Samuel 23^2).
'Now', said Isaiah, 'the Lord and His Spirit hath sent
me' (Isaiah 48^{16}: 'The Lord God hath sent me and His
Spirit', RSV).

The given message may be a message of comfort and of
consolation and of promise. 'The Spirit of the Lord is upon
me', said Isaiah, 'because the Lord hath anointed me to
preach good tidings unto the meek; He hath sent me to bind
up the broken-hearted, to proclaim liberty to the captives,

and the opening of the prison to them that are bound' (Isaiah 61[1]). It may be a message of warning, rebuke and threat. 'I am full of power', said Micah, 'by the Spirit of the Lord . . . to declare unto Jacob his transgression and unto Israel his sin' (Micah 3[8]). The message of the Spirit is no one-toned, monotonous proclamation; the voice of the Spirit has always the accent men need to hear. The message of the Spirit is no orthodox irrelevancy; it is always a tract for the times. Men disregard that prophetic voice of the Spirit at their peril. It was Zechariah's announcement that the wrath of the Lord of hosts was great, because the people had made their hearts as adamant, 'lest they should hear the law, and the words which the Lord of hosts sent in His Spirit by the former prophets' (Zechariah 7[12]).

There is a series of passages in the works of the Chronicler which shows the Spirit of the Lord giving to prophetic men a message for a moment when affairs were on the razor's edge. When David was still a fugitive, and when his fortunes were still uncertain, there came to him the mighty men. He asked whether they came in peace or in enmity; and the Spirit of the Lord came upon Amasai to pledge their loyalty to David (1 Chronicles 12[1-18]). In the days of Asa, when Israel had been for long 'without the true God, without a teaching priest, and without the law', the Spirit of God came upon Azariah to summon men back to God (2 Chronicles 15[1-7]). When Jehosaphat and the people were in fear because of the Moabites and the Ammonites, the Spirit of the Lord came upon Jahaziel to bring a message of courage and of hope (2 Chronicles 20[1-19]).

It is the Spirit of God who uses men to bring to other men a message for the times. No man who asks for, and receives, the guidance of the Spirit can ever be an irrelevant teacher or preacher. The Spirit of God is always looking for men who will be messengers to their day and generation. There is no moment without its message from God, there is no crisis without its word, if a man can be found by the Spirit to bring that message and that word.

There is no prophet in whom the work of the Spirit is more constant and vivid and illuminating than Ezekiel. The Spirit of the Lord gave Ezekiel *his commission and his message*. 'The Spirit of the Lord fell on me, and said: Speak' (Ezekiel 11[5]). The Spirit of the Lord gave Ezekiel *courage to face the message and the situation*. 'The Spirit entered into me . . . and set me on my feet' (Ezekiel 2[2]). The Spirit of the Lord promised Ezekiel *strength and power to obey His own commands*. 'I will put my Spirit within you', said God, 'and cause you to walk in my statutes, and ye shall keep my judgements, and do them' (Ezekiel 36[27]).

It is the conviction of the Old Testament that no man can prophesy without the Spirit. No man can teach others unless he himself be taught. The Spirit is God's witness in any human situation. It is through the Spirit that with the need there always comes the power. And it is the Spirit who gives the prophet the strength and the courage to bring to men the message of God, whether that message be consolation or condemnation.

(4) Great as is the work of the Spirit in the Old Testament, the fact remains that *in general the work of the Spirit is connected with the extraordinary and the abnormal*. The work of the Spirit is not so much a daily power and presence as it is an abnormal phenomenon and manifestation.

The tremendous feats of strength of Samson are attributed to the Spirit of the Lord (Judges 13[25], 14[6, 19], 15[14]). It is not everyday life with which the Spirit is connected, but with the unrepeatable moments. Even in the case of prophecy, the prophecy in the early times tends to be ecstatic and abnormal. When Saul prophesied, he stripped off his clothes, and lay down naked all that day and all that night (1 Samuel 19[24]). The work of the Spirit is connected more with the moment of ecstasy than with the daily routine.

The manifestations of the Spirit are wonderful and miraculous. When Obadiah meets Elijah, Elijah tells him to go and tell Ahab that Elijah is here. Obadiah objects because 'as soon as I am gone from thee, the Spirit of the Lord shall carry thee whither I know not', and Ahab will think the message false and will slay him (1 Kings 18⁷⁻¹⁶). When Elijah vanishes from the sight of men, the sons of the prophets suggest to Elisha that they should go and search for him, 'lest peradventure the Spirit of the Lord hath taken him up and cast him upon some mountain, or into some valley' (2 Kings 2¹⁶). Repeatedly Ezekiel speaks about being taken up by the Spirit and moved hither and thither. 'He put forth the form of an hand, and took me by a lock of mine head; and the Spirit lifted me up between the earth and heaven (Ezekiel 8³; cf. 3¹², ¹⁴, 11¹, ²⁴, 43⁵).

In the Old Testament the tendency is for the Spirit to be the privilege of the prophet, and that sometimes in the moment of ecstasy. The experience of the Spirit is not an experience for the common man or for the every day. In the case of the earlier prophets the manifestations of the Spirit tend to be inexplicable and extraordinary and not to be re-captured in life's ordinary routine. Although, as we shall see, it is not always so, the fact remains that the general idea of the Old Testament is that the work of the Spirit is neither for the ordinary man nor for the ordinary occasion, but for the extraordinary man and the abnormal occasion.

(5) It is nevertheless true that it is possible to overstress the element of abnormality in the idea of the working of the Spirit in the Old Testament. It may be that in the early days and the primitive thinking the abnormality is there; but there is much more than that in the highest thought of the Old Testament. *The Spirit stands for the universal presence of God.* The Spirit stands for the fact that it is neither possible to lose God in trouble nor to escape God in sin. 'Whither shall I go from Thy Spirit', says the Psalmist, 'or whither shall I flee from Thy presence?' (Psalm 139⁷). The heavens, the earth and the underworld are all full of the Spirit of God. 'The Spirit of God', says the writer of the Wisdom of Solomon, 'hath filled the world, and that which holdeth all things together hath knowledge of every voice. Therefore, no man that uttereth unrighteous things shall be unseen' (Wisdom of

Solomon 1⁷). The Spirit of God makes the world the dwelling place of God.

(6) In a very special sense, because Israel is the people of God, *Israel is the people amidst whom the Spirit of God dwells.* If the Spirit of God has a home upon earth, that home is amidst the fellowship of the people of God. When the people were in the desert the Spirit was with them. It was then that the Spirit dwelt amidst them, and gave them strength for the journey and rest on the way. 'Where is He who put in the midst of them His Holy Spirit? . . . Like cattle who go down in the valley, the Spirit of the Lord gave them rest' (Isaiah 63¹¹⁻¹⁴, RSV). It was part of the covenant that the Spirit would rest in the midst of Israel. 'Take courage all you people of the land', says Haggai, 'work, for I am with you, says the Lord of hosts, according to the promise that I made with you, when you came out of Egypt. My Spirit abides among you; fear not' (Haggai 2⁴, ⁵, RSV). 'As for me' Isaiah hears God say, 'this is my covenant with them: my Spirit which is upon you, and my words which I have put in your mouth, shall not depart out of your mouth, or out of the mouth of your children, or out of the mouth of your children's children, says the Lord, from this time forth and for evermore' (Isaiah 59²¹, RSV).

In the fellowship of the people of God the Spirit dwells. The Church is the new Israel, and for us the Church should be the Spirit-filled community of the people of God.

(7) It is a natural corollary to this that the age of God, the golden age, the time to come, the Messianic days, will be a time of a special outpouring of the Spirit. Of the Messianic king himself it is said, 'The Spirit of the Lord shall rest upon him' (Isaiah 11²). The promise of God is, 'I will pour my Spirit upon thy seed, and my blessing upon thine offspring' (Isaiah 44³). The promise through Ezekiel is, 'I will not hide my face any more from them, when I pour out my Spirit upon the house of Israel, says the Lord God' (Ezekiel 39²⁹). In Joel the great promise of the age of God is, 'I will pour out my Spirit upon all flesh' (Joel 2²⁸). The age of God is the age of the Spirit. No new world can be made, and no new age can

dawn, unless the Spirit of God comes upon men. All the planning of men may change the world and still leave it as it is; the only power which can re-create the world as it now is into the world which is the dream of God and the desire of men is the power of the Spirit.

(8) We have kept to the end one function of the Spirit in the Old Testament which is different from the others, and which is yet of great significance. More than once, in the story of the making of the Tabernacle, when arrangements are being made that all should be as beautiful and as fitting as possible, a certain name occurs. It is the name of a man called Bezaleel. God bade Moses set this man aside for the work, because 'I have filled him with the Spirit of God, in wisdom, and in understanding, and in knowledge, and in all manner of workmanship, to devise cunning works, to work in gold, and in silver, and in brass, and in cutting of stones, to set them, and in carving of timber, to work in all manner of workmanship' (Exodus 31[1-5]; cf. 35[31], 36[1]). Here is something new. *Craftsmanship is the gift of the Spirit.* Here is something which in an illuminating flash transfers the Spirit from the realm of theology to the realm of life, from the stillness of the Church to crash of the hammer and the buzz of the saw and the noise of the chisel on the stone in the workshop. Here the Spirit is indeed in the midst of life and living. We do well to remember that, whatever gift a man has, of mind or heart, of brain or eye or hand, that gift is the gift of the Spirit. It is not only the theologian in his study, the priest in his church, the prophet with his message, who is working in the power of the Spirit; the man at the bench and at the machine, the man in whose hands wood and metal become obedient, the mechanic, the engineer, the carpenter, the fitter, the mason, are all men of the Spirit, and can, and must, serve God in the Spirit.

Such, then, is the Old Testament background of thought about the Spirit. Already there is greatness and nobility there, and it is on that foundation that the New Testament goes on to build a still greater structure of thought and of belief in the Spirit.

CHAPTER TWO

The Holy Spirit in the first three Gospels

WHEN WE begin to study the material about the Holy Spirit in the first three Gospels, the first thing that strikes us is the meagreness of the material, for in these Gospels the references to the Spirit are few and far between. But, even if the actual references are few, the meanings which emerge from them are of the utmost importance. The material falls into four broad sections.

(1) There are the events which preceded the birth of Jesus. This material we find in the first two chapters of Luke's Gospel; and in the brief references within these chapters we get a cameo-like summary of the work of the Spirit.

(a) We come again on the old prophetic work of the Spirit. It is because he is full of the Spirit that Zacharias prophesies (Luke 1⁶⁷). It is because she was full of the Spirit that Elisabeth broke out into her great hymn of praise to Mary (Luke 1⁴¹). The Spirit is still the messenger of God to men.

(b) But it is in the case of Simeon that we receive in four short verses a perfect illustration of the work of the Spirit, as Jewish men of devotion saw and experienced that work.

Simeon was a man upon whom the Holy Spirit rested (Luke 2²⁵). It was the Spirit who *revealed* the truth of God to Simeon, that he should see the Lord's Anointed before he died (Luke 2²⁶). It was the Spirit who *guided* Simeon to the place where he might find that truth (Luke 2²⁷), for it was the Spirit who brought Simeon into the Temple on the day when His parents brought the infant Jesus there. And it was the Spirit who enabled Simeon to *recognize* the truth of God when he was confronted with it. Here is a complete summary of the Jewish belief in the Spirit. The Spirit reveals God's truth to men; the Spirit confronts men with that truth; and the Spirit enables them to recognize and to understand that truth when they do see it. To this we must later return, but at the moment we note only that for a Jew this is a perfect summary of the work of the Spirit, and it is so for us today. It is the Spirit who reveals God's truth to men; it is the Spirit who brings men into the presence of that truth; it is the Spirit who enables men to recognize the truth when they see it. It is clear that men can neither find nor recognize God's truth without the help of God's Spirit.

(2) There is the place of the Spirit in the life of Jesus Himself. Every part of Jesus' earthly life is intimately connected with the Spirit.

(a) It was the Spirit who gave Him birth and through whose work He entered into this world of space and time. 'The Holy Spirit', said Gabriel to Mary, 'shall come upon thee' (Luke 1[35]). 'Mary', says Matthew, 'was found with child by the Holy Spirit' (Matthew 1[18]). 'That which is conceived in her', said the angel to Joseph, 'is of the Holy Spirit' (Matthew 1[20]). It is well to note that, when we say this, we are not necessarily committing ourselves to an implicit belief in the Virgin Birth. It is not every act of intercourse which begets a child; and it was Jewish belief that no child ever came into this world without the work of the Spirit of God. 'There are three partners in the production of any human being', runs the Jewish saying, 'the Holy One, blessed is He, the father and the mother' (*Niddah* 31a). No matter what belief we may hold about the birth of Jesus, whether we hold to the Virgin Birth, or whether we think of the birth of Jesus as a natural birth, the fact of the work of the Holy Spirit in it remains unaltered and unchanged. If the Spirit of God was operative in the creation of the world (Genesis 1[2]), then that same Spirit is supremely operative in the recreation of the world. If the Spirit of God has been throughout all ages God's messenger to men, then that same Spirit is uniquely operative and effective in the coming of Him who is God's final message to men.

(b) It was by the Spirit that Jesus was equipped for His

task in the world. At His Baptism the Spirit came upon Jesus in all His fulness and His power (Matthew 3[16]; Mark 1[10]; Luke 3[22]; John 1[32, 33]). It was in Jesus that the prophetic word about the Servant of God was perfectly fulfilled: 'Behold my Servant. . . . I have put my Spirit upon Him (Isaiah 42[1]). For thirty years Jesus had waited patiently in Nazareth (Luke 3[23]). Now for Him God's hour had struck; and the first event which happened to Him as He laid His hand to God's task was the coming of the Spirit upon Him. No man, not even the Son of God, can do God's work without God's Spirit. All the human equipment that the workman of God can have for his work is useless without the equipment of the Spirit.

(c) Luke tells us that Jesus was full of the Spirit (Luke 4[1]). When it is used of Jesus, this phrase has a special and a unique meaning. All the great prophets and the great men of God received their message from the Spirit. But great as they were, their experience of the Spirit was transitory and spasmodic; with them the Spirit ebbed and flowed. They received the Spirit for special and particular tasks and for special and particular messages. But for Jesus the Spirit was a lasting, permanent, abiding, inalienable equipment. What they had at sundry times and in divers manners, what they had in a measure that was partial and fragmentary and impermanent, He had for ever.

(d) It was the Spirit who guided Jesus and who directed His life and actions. It was the Spirit who lead Him into the wilderness to be tested by the devil (Matthew 4[1]; Mark 1[12]; Luke 4[1]), and it was in the power of the Spirit that He returned to Galilee (Luke 4[14]). When we follow the life of Jesus, we see that there is a certainty in it. His course is undeviating, like an arrow to its target. There are no deflections, no oscillations, no waverings, no uncertainties. Upon Him and within Him there was the Spirit, the messenger of God, guide and director of His life.

(e) It was the Spirit who empowered Jesus. 'If I cast out devils', said Jesus, 'by the Spirit of God then is the Kingdom, of God come unto you' (Matthew 12[28]). It is significant to note that Luke transmits that saying in a different form: 'If I with *the finger of God* cast out devils, then no doubt the Kingdom of God is come upon you' (Luke 11²⁰). It is quite unnecessary to argue as to which of these two forms of the saying is original and genuine. In this case we are confronted not with an *either or* but with a *both and*. It is far more probable that this is something which Jesus said far more than once, and that He used both forms of the saying.

For Jesus *the Spirit of God* and the vivid phrase *the finger of God* meant the same thing. It is of the utmost significance to note that this phrase *the finger of God* occurs in the Old Testament in three connections. It occurs in connection with *the creating work of God*. The heavens are the works of God's fingers (Psalm 8³). It occurs in connection with *the revealing work of God*. The tables of the Ten Commandments are written by the finger of God (Exodus 31¹⁸; Deuteronomy 9¹⁰). It occurs in connection with *the demonstration of the power of God* for the deliverance of His people. The reaction of the Egyptian magicians to the wonders which preceded the exodus is: 'This is the finger of God' (Exodus 8¹⁹).

When Jesus speaks of the finger of God, the Spirit of God, acting through Him, it means that in Him there came to its consummation the creating, the revealing, and the redeeming power of God.

(3) There is the place of the Spirit in the life of the followers of Jesus. It must be clear that if Jesus was dependent on the Spirit, His followers must be even more dependent.

(a) It was John the Baptist's reaction to say that Jesus was to baptize men, not in water, but with the Spirit (Matthew 3¹¹; Mark 1⁸; Luke 3¹⁶; John 1³³). The Greek is *en pneumati hagiō*. Certainly this can mean *with the Spirit* as the Authorized Version, the Revised Version, the Revised Standard Version, and Moffatt all take it. But it is equally possible that this phrase can mean *in the Spirit* as Rieu and Weymouth both take it. The verb *to baptize* is *baptizein*, which ordinarily means *to dip*. There is a vivid picture here. The Christian is a man who is dipped in the Spirit. The verb *baptizein* can be used of dipping garments to dye them. The Christian is a man who is dyed through and through with the Spirit. He is a man whose whole life is soaked in the Spirit, a man the colour of whose whole life is changed by the Spirit. The Christian is a Spirit-anointed, Spirit-dipped, Spirit-saturated, Spirit-dominated man. And the drabness of life, and the inadequacy of life, and the futility of life, and the earthboundness of life, which characterize so many of us, all come from the failure to submit to that baptism of the Spirit which Christ alone can give.

(b) The Spirit is the essence of all God's good gifts to men, who are His children. 'If ye then being evil', says Jesus, 'know how to give good gifts unto your children, how much more shall your heavenly Father give the Holy Spirit to them that ask Him?' (Luke 11[13]). It is again to be noted that Matthew transmits this saying differently. In his version the last phrase reads: 'How much more will your heavenly Father give *good things* to them that ask Him?' (Matthew 7[11]). Once again, we do not need to make choice between alternatives. We may well hold that Jesus used both forms of this saying, and that in so doing He was saying both that the Spirit of God is God's supreme gift to men, and that through the Spirit of God all good gifts come to men.

(c) The Spirit is the Christian's ally in time of need. When the Christian is faced with persecution and with danger, when he is in peril of his life and in peril of his faith, he need not be anxious, for in that same hour the Holy Spirit will tell him what to say and what to do (Matthew 10[20]; Mark 13[11]; Luke 12[12]). The Christian is never left to battle alone; the help of the Spirit will enable him to face the unfaceable and to do the undoable and to bear the unbearable.

(d) The Church is to be the channel through which the Spirit comes to men. As Matthew has it, the commission of the disciples is that they must go out and baptize men in the name of the Father and of the Son and of the Holy Spirit (Matthew 28[19]). It is needless to discuss whether we have here a verbatim report of a word of Jesus. This is beyond doubt the conception of the task of the Church which Jesus left to His men, whether the actual words are His or not. The task of Spirit-filled men is to make a Spirit-filled world. He who has received the gift of the Spirit well knows that he must be the channel of God whereby the Spirit comes to others.

(4) The material of the first three Gospels confronts us with one other aspect of the Holy Spirit—the sin against the Holy Spirit. It may well be said that this is the most terrifying thought in the New Testament. There are those whose permanent accent is condemnation, and whose habitual tone is anger, but to find a saying like this on the lips of Him who was the incarnate love of God sends a shiver into the heart and into the soul. It is little wonder that there are those who have lost their reason because they have become obsessed with this saying of Jesus. We may best get at the meaning of it by approaching it along three avenues.

(a) The form of the saying is uncertain, and we must first try to discover what is the original of it. Let us set it down as each of the Gospel writers tell it to us.

Verily I say unto you, all sins shall be forgiven unto the sons of men, and blasphemies wherewithsoever they shall blaspheme, but he that shall blaspheme against the Holy Spirit hath never forgiveness, but is in danger of eternal damnation (Mark 3$^{28-9}$).

Wherefore I say unto you, All manner of sin and blasphemy shall be forgiven unto men, but the blasphemy against the Holy Spirit shall not be forgiven unto men. And whosoever speaketh a word against the Son of Man, it shall be forgiven him, but whosoever speaketh against the Holy Spirit, it shall not be forgiven him, neither in this world, neither in the world to come (Matthew 12$^{31-2}$).

And whosoever shall speak a word against the Son of Man, it shall be forgiven him, but unto him that blasphemeth against the Holy Spirit it shall not be forgiven (Luke 12^{10}).

Two facts about the form of this saying are strange. First, Mark has nothing to say about the sin against the Son of Man. Second, it seems very strange to say with such deliberation that a sin against the Son of Man, that is, against Jesus, is less serious than a sin against the Holy Spirit, for it is the teaching of the whole New Testament that it is precisely a man's re-action to Jesus which settles his destiny in time and in eternity. In fact, Luke immediately before he records the saying about the sin against the Holy Spirit records Jesus' saying that He will confess before God him who confesses Him on earth, and He will deny before God him who denies Him upon earth (Luke 12[8-9]).

This twofold strangeness makes us wonder if there may not be something wrong with the form in which the saying has come down to us. In ordinary Hebrew and Aramaic the phrase *a son of man* is simply the expression for *a man*. Again and again God addresses Ezekiel as 'Son of Man' (Ezekiel 2[1, 3, 6], 3[1, 4]). The Psalmist asks: 'What is man that Thou art mindful of him? and the son of man that Thou visitest him?' (Psalm 8[3]); and there quite clearly *man* and *son of man* mean the same thing. When the Rabbis began their parables and stories, they regularly began: 'There was a son of man . . .', where we should begin: 'There was a man . . .' It may well be that in Matthew's and Luke's version of Jesus' saying about the sin against the Holy Spirit, the reference is not to a sin or a blasphemy or a word against *the Son of Man*, but to a sin or blasphemy or word against *a son of man*. It may well be that what Jesus is saying is this: 'It is quite forgivable to speak a word against, to disbelieve, to disobey, to slander *a man*, because any man is fallible and any man can be misunderstood, but it is unforgivable to speak against, or to disbelieve, or to slander, or to resist the Holy Spirit, whose voice carries all the conviction of the truth of God.' It may be that Jesus is saying: 'You may disregard the voice of a man and escape the consequences of such a denial, but you can never disregard the voice of the Holy Spirit and escape the consequences of such a denial.'

(b) Second, we must look at the context of this saying. In Luke it has no context; it is an unrelated saying. In Matthew and in Mark it has the same context. Jesus has just healed a man who was possessed by a devil. The Jewish authorities did not deny the cure; but they ascribed it to the fact that Jesus was in league with the devil, that Jesus cast out devils by the help of the prince of the devils. That is to say, these Jewish Scribes and Pharisees could look at incarnate goodness and call it the work of the devil; they could look at action which was Godlike and call it devilish. It is in face of that situation that Jesus uttered this saying.

(c) It must be clear that when Jesus uttered this saying, He meant it to be understood in *Jewish* terms. He was speaking to Jews, who knew nothing of the Christian belief in the Holy Spirit. Pentecost and all its wonder had not yet come. We are bound to interpret the work of the Holy Spirit in the light of Jewish thought in this passage, for it is only in that light that the people to whom Jesus was speaking knew the Holy Spirit. We have already seen that for a Jew the great work of the Holy Spirit was twofold: the Holy Spirit brought God's truth to men, and the Holy Spirit enabled men to recognize that truth when they were confronted with it.

It is a fact of life that, if a man for long enough refuses to use a faculty, he will end by losing it. The classic example of that comes from the life of Darwin. In his youth Darwin loved poetry and music. He spent so much time on biology that in the end he lost completely the power to read poetry or to appreciate music. And he said that, if he were beginning life over again, he would read a little poetry each day and listen to a little music each day, so that he would not lose the power to know and to love and to appreciate them. Again, it is a fact of life that this is tragically true of sin. The first time a man commits a sin, he does so with a shudder in the soul, a hating of self, a piercing realization that he is doing the wrong thing. If he commits the sin a second time, it is easier; he finds within himself less resistance to it. And in the end he can reach a state when the sinful act leaves him unmoved, and when he can even fail to recognize it as sinful.

Now let us return to the Jews to whom Jesus had spoken. All their lives and all through their history God had been speaking to them, appealing to them, offering them His truth and His revelation. But the fact was that they had so long shut their ears to that voice, refused that guidance, been blind to that truth, that when God incarnate came to them they utterly failed to realize who He was and to recognize Him, and even saw in Him the work of the devil. They had so long chosen their own way, the wrong way, that in the end good seemed to them evil and evil seemed to them good. *That is the sin against the Holy Spirit.* The Holy Spirit is He who enables men to recognize the truth of God when they see it. But, if a man for long enough deliberately shuts his eyes to the truth, then in the end he loses the ability to recognize it when he sees it, and then he has committed the sin against the Holy Spirit.

Why should that be the *unforgivable* sin? If a man cannot recognize goodness when he sees it, then he does not even know when he is sinning. If by his repeated acts of the rejection of the will of God, he has reached this stage, *then repentance becomes impossible*, because goodness has lost its fascination and evil has lost its horror. And if a man cannot repent, he cannot be forgiven. It is not God who has shut the door; the man has shut it on himself.

Here, then, is the meaning of the sin against the Holy Spirit. and from all this two things emerge clearly.

The first is a comfort which might have saved many a tortured heart from its self-accusing agony. The one man who cannot possibly have committed the sin against the Holy Spirit is the man who fears that he has. If a man has committed the sin against the Holy Spirit, he has lost the sense of sin. No man who knows himself to be a sinner has committed the sin against the Holy Spirit.

The second is a solemn reminder. The one way never to be in any danger of committing the sin against the Holy Spirit is to keep ourselves sensitive to the voice of God. He who lives close to Christ, constant in prayer, diligent in the study of God's word, ever mindful of Him in whom he lives and moves and has his being, can never commit the sin against the Holy Spirit, for such a man is always ready to listen to God's truth, and to recognize it when he sees it.

CHAPTER THREE

The Holy Spirit in the Fourth Gospel

WHEN WE come to the Fourth Gospel, we come to the high-water mark of the teaching of the New Testament about the Holy Spirit. It is the words of the Fourth Gospel which have coloured all our thinking about the Spirit, and which have given us our deepest and our most precious beliefs about the Spirit.

We may begin our study of the material of the Fourth Gospel by turning to what is on the surface the most startling thing that it says about the Spirit. John tells us of the great promise of Jesus to give the living water which can quench the thirst of the soul (John 7$^{37-8}$). That promise was given under the most dramatic of circumstances. John tells us that on the last great day of the feast Jesus stood and cried: 'If any man thirst, let him come to me and drink' (John 7^{37}). When we read the narrative a little further back, we find that these words were spoken in the Temple court (John 7^{14}). The feast in question was the Feast of Tabernacles. The Feast of Tabernacles was one of the most joyful of all Jewish festivals. It was a harvest-thanksgiving festival, and it was also a commemoration of the days when the people journeyed through the wilderness to the promised land. It was because of that commemoration that it received its name, for throughout it the people dwelt in little booths or tabernacles made of branches of trees to remind them of the days when they had dwelt in tents on the long journey from Egypt to Palestine.

The most moving and dramatic ceremony of this feast came upon the last day. On that day the Temple courts were thronged with people and the streets were lined with spectators. The High Priest took from the Temple a silver pitcher

which held about two pints of water. In procession he carried
the pitcher through the crowded streets to the Pool of Siloam.
There he filled it with water, and carried it back through the
crowds to the Temple. While this was being done, the people
joyfully chanted the promise which God made to Isaiah:
'With joy shall ye draw water out of the wells of salvation'
(Isaiah 12³), which was a promise and a forecast of the wonder
of the time when the Messiah would come. When the priest
had carried the pitcher of water back to the crowd-packed
Temple courts, he took it to the altar of the burnt-offering and
flung the water on to the altar as an offering to God.

The symbolism of this ceremony is clear; it had a threefold
impact, of every part of which the thronging people were very
conscious. First, it was a thanksgiving for God's good gift
of water, in memory of the waterless and thirsty days in the
desert. Second, it was what might be called an acted prayer
for rain, so that the harvest would never fail. Third, it was a
forecast of the days of the Messiah, when God's people would
draw water from the wells of salvation, and when God's Spirit
would be poured into the thirsty souls of men.

It may well have been at the very moment when the water
was being poured upon the altar, that the voice of Jesus rang
through the Temple courts: 'If any man thirst, let him come
to me and drink.' Jesus was saying: 'You are thanking God
for the water, of which if a man drink, he will thirst again;
I can give you the living water which can quench the un-
satisfied longings of your souls. You are dreaming of the days
of the Messiah, when the Spirit of God will be poured out
upon men; these days have come.' There is no more dramatic
scene in all the New Testament story.

It is then that John adds his comment. He explains that
Jesus was talking of the Spirit; and then he says: 'The Spirit
was not yet, because that Jesus was not yet glorified' (John
7³⁹). The Authorized Version has it: 'The Spirit was not yet
given.' But even in the Authorized Version the word *given* is
printed in italics to show that it has no direct equivalent in
the Greek. The Revised Version and the Revised Standard

Version retain the translation of the Authorized Version. Moffatt has: 'As yet there was no Spirit, because Jesus had not been glorified yet.' There is no doubt that in the oldest and the best Greek manuscripts of the New Testament the word *given* is not in the text (*oupō gar ēn pneuma, hoti Iēsous oudepō edoxasthē*).

The startling feature about this comment of John is that it seems on the face of it to say that the Holy Spirit did not come into existence until after the glorification and ascension of Jesus Christ, which would present an insoluble problem for the doctrine of the Trinity. But that is not what John means; he has already spoken of the descent of the Spirit upon Jesus at His Baptism (1[32]), and he has already shown us Jesus telling Nicodemus that a man must be born again from above of water and of the Spirit (3[5, 6]). What John means is that only after the glorification and ascension of Jesus did the Spirit descend upon men in all His plenitude and power, that it was only after the return of Jesus to glory that the event of Pentecost took place. If often happens that at some given point in time, and because of some action and event, men enter into a completely new experience of something which has already for long existed. The power may always have existed, but it required someone's action or discovery to release its flood-tides upon men. That is the way in which men entered into the experience of the Spirit; and that leads us straight to the greatest teaching about the Spirit in the New Testament, the 14th, 15th and 16th chapters of John's Gospel, for these are the chapters which tell of the coming parting from Jesus in the flesh, and the coming presence of the Spirit among men. So, then, to these chapters let us turn.

John has his own distinctive title for the Spirit; he calls the Spirit the *paraklētos*, the Paraclete (John 14[16], 14[26], 15[26], 16[7]). This is the word which the Authorized Version translates *Comforter*, and that is a very unfortunate translation, for it tends to limit the work of the Holy Spirit to comfort and consolation in the time of trouble and of distress. *Paraklētos* is no easy word to translate, as the efforts of modern translators show. The Revised Version retains *Comforter* in the text, but notes that the Greek is *paraclete* and in the margin suggests *advocate* and *helper*. The Revised Standard Version uses *counsellor*; J. B. Phillips translates it *someone to stand by you*; C. Kingsley Williams translates it *the Friend*; Ronald Knox translates it *He who is to befriend you*; Moffatt, Torrey and the Twentieth Century New Testament all translate it *Helper*. The number of different translations shows the difficulty of finding an equivalent for the word and the wealth of meaning that is in it.

Let us begin by examining the translation *Comforter*, and by seeing how it arose and what it really means. The translation *Comforter* goes back to Wiclif; but he was not using it in the narrow sense of a comforter and consoler in sorrow. Wiclif translates Ephesians 6[10]: 'Be ye *comforted* in the Lord.' There the word *to comfort* is *endunamoun*, which is derived from the Greek word *dunamis* which means *power*, and which comes from the same root as the English word *dynamite*. Tyndale retranslated Ephesians 6[10]: 'Be strong in the Lord', a translation which the Authorized Version retains. This same word *endunamoun* occurs again in 1 Timothy 1[12], where again Wiclif translates: 'I do thankings to Him who *comforted* me.' Here Tyndale has: 'I thank Him who has *made me strong*,' and the Authorized Version has: 'I thank Him who *hath enabled me*.' The basic fact is that when Wiclif used the word *Comforter*, he was using it in its literal sense. It is derived from the Latin word *fortis*, which means *brave*, and for Wiclif *Comforter* did not mean simply one who tenderly and sympathetically consoles in sorrow; it meant one who puts courage into us, one who enables us to be brave, one who empowers us to cope with the chances and the changes and the struggles and the battles of this life. Time has narrowed the meaning of the word *Comforter*, but the word was intended to mean that the Holy Spirit gives us strength and courage to meet the demands of this exacting life.

Let us, then, still further attempt to get at the meaning of this great word. *Paraklētos* comes from the word *parakalein*;

parakalein means *to call to one's side; paraklētos*, therefore, means *someone who is called to one's side*. But called for what purpose? *Parakalein* is used of calling some one in as an *ally*, as a *counsellor*, of inviting some one to *lend his assistance* with some great task. Above all, *parakalein* is used of calling in someone as a *witness* in one's favour, and as an *advocate* in one's cause. When the Jews in Alexandria were oppressed and ill-treated, they sought to find a *paraklētos* to plead their cause with Gaius the Roman Emperor (Philo, *In Flaccum*, 4). The Jewish Rabbis took over this word and transliterated it into Hebrew letters, and they said that every good deed a man ever did would one day be his *paraklētos* in the presence of the judgement of God. At a court-martial there is someone there to defend the man on trial, and he is called *the prisoner's friend*; that is precisely what the word *paraklētos* meant.

There are two further strands of meaning which we must weave into this pattern. On rare occasions the word *parakalein* does mean *to comfort*. For instance, in the Septuagint it is the word which is used in Isaiah 40$^{1-2}$: '*Comfort ye, comfort ye* my people, saith your God.' But even then the comfort is not of such a kind that it enables a man passively and dully to bear his trial, but of such a kind that it enables a man to stand on his own two feet and to face life with steady eyes.

Further, *parakalein* is regularly used for exhorting and encouraging the man who is going into battle. Aeschylus, describing a naval battle, says: 'The long galleys cheered [*parakalein*] each other line by line' (*Persae*, 380), and Polybius uses it of a general putting fire and courage into dejected troops before they face a battle against desperate odds (3. 19, 40).

Here, then, is something of the magnificent wealth and splendour of this word. To call the Holy Spirit *paraklētos* is to say that the Holy Spirit is the person who enables a man to meet four-square and erect the sorrows, the struggles, the burdens of this world, the person who nerves the feeble for the battle and who makes the coward brave, the person who gives us wise counsel and powerful help in the difficult decisions of life, the person who is for us the prisoner's friend when we face

the judgement of God. When we think of all that, we can do
no other than pray: 'God, send Thy Holy Spirit upon *me*.'

We must now examine in detail the teaching of John's three
chapters about the Holy Spirit.

(1) The Holy Spirit is the gift of God in Jesus Christ
'I will pray the Father', said Jesus, 'and He will give you
another Comforter' (14^{15}). He speaks of the Comforter whom
He will send from the Father (15^{26}). It is well to remember
that the possession of the Holy Spirit is a gift and not an
achievement. He who would receive the Spirit must learn to
wait upon God. 'Be still', said the Psalmist, 'and know that I
am God' (Psalm 46^{10}). 'Stand still', said Moses to the fear-
stricken people, when the avenging Pharaoh pursued them,
'and see the salvation of the Lord' (Exodus 14^{13}). It is the
tragedy of life that so many are too busy to give God the chance
to send His Spirit to them.

(2) The Holy Spirit is the abiding presence of the Risen
Lord. 'It is expedient for you that I go away:', said Jesus, 'for
if I go not away, the Comforter will not come unto you; but if
I depart, I will send him unto you' (16^7). 'I will pray the
Father,' said Jesus, 'and he shall give you another Comforter,
that he may abide with you for ever' (14^{16}). In 14^{18} the
Authorized Version translates: 'I will not leave you comfort-
less: *I will come to you*', but the Greek of the last phrase is not,
'I will come to you', but 'I am coming to you'. The promise
is of perpetual and continual and uninterrupted coming.

The truth, paradoxical as it may sound, is that Jesus had
to go away from His people in order to be for ever present
with them in His Spirit. So long as the Incarnation lasted, so
long as Jesus was here in the flesh, He was subject to all the
laws of space and time. He could only be in one place, and
with one group of people, at a time. Fellowship with Him was
necessarily a thing of coming and going, of meeting and
parting. But once He was rid of the limitations of the body,
He was able to be everywhere and at all times present with
His people in His Spirit. As Westcott puts it: 'The withdrawal
of the limited bodily presence necessarily prepared the way

for the recognition of a universal presence.' And as Gore puts it: 'The coming of the Holy Spirit was not merely to supply the absence of the Son but to complete His presence.' Body is subject to all the limiting laws of the body; Spirit is emancipated from the body's limitations. 'I was in the isle that is called Patmos. . . . I was in the Spirit on the Lord's day', writes the John of the Revelation (Revelation 1[9]). Patmos might be a little island in the Mediterranean Sea; it might be a foreign land and a place of exile; it might be a penal settlement where John worked in chains in the quarries but there he was in the Spirit. Because of the coming of the Spirit there is no place in all the world where a man can be separated from Jesus Christ.

(3) And yet there is something to add to this. Jesus said: 'If ye love me, keep my commandments. And I will pray the Father, and He shall give you another Comforter.' And then He went on to tell how the world cannot receive the Spirit, because it neither knows not sees Him (14[16-17]). The Spirit comes to him who loves God, and who keeps God's commandments. In John's writings, the world, as Gore defined it, is human nature organizing itself without God. The coming of the Spirit is not absolutely unconditional. There can be no fellowship between those who are diametrically opposed; even if a person seeks for, and longs for, and poignantly desires fellowship with another, that fellowship is impossible if the other ignores the very existence of him who desires fellowship. There is a certain courtesy in God, which makes Him refrain from forcing Himself upon the man who does not want Him. The Spirit comes to him who waits on God, to him who seeks —even amidst failure—to live close to God. To receive the Spirit we must first desire the Spirit. To live in the world in the power of the Spirit, we must at least sometimes withdraw from the world to receive the Spirit. Righteousness is for those who hunger and thirst after it (Matthew 5[6]). A man can come to a stage when he is so immersed in the world that the immortal longings of his soul have ceased to be, and when he is so earthbound that he forgets the things beyond the horizons

of this world. To such a man the Spirit cannot come; but to any man in whose heart there is the longing for God—even amidst his sin—the Spirit comes.

(4) John's favourite title for, and description of, the Spirit is the Spirit of Truth (14[17], 15[26], 16[13]). The Spirit and the truth are intimately related and connected.

(a) The Spirit is the *teacher* of truth. 'He will teach you all things', said Jesus (14[26]). By far the most interesting and important saying about the Spirit's teaching office is in 16[13]. The Authorized Version translates that passage: 'He will lead you into all truth.' The more modern versions, Revised Version, Revised Standard Version, Moffatt and Kingsley Williams, translate: 'He will lead you into all the truth.' Rieu has: 'He will lead you into truth entire.' There are two great truths here.

First, the Spirit of God leads us into the whole truth. Our unaided minds can grasp and discover only partial and fragmentary truths; by ourselves we have to be satisfied with guessings and gropings after the truth. It is through the Spirit alone that we enter into the full orb of truth. It is the Spirit who enables us to find 'the truth, the whole truth, and nothing but the truth'. That is why strenuous thinking by itself can lead only to frustration and bewilderment; that is why the mind by itself can produce more problems than solutions; and that is why thinking and waiting, and thinking and praying, must always go hand in hand.

Second, the Spirit of God leads us into all truth. This means that every discovery in every sphere of truth that men have made is the work of the Spirit. Nothing could be more wrong than to limit the guidance of the Spirit to what we might call theological truth. Every great poem, every great piece of music, every scientific discovery is the work of the Spirit. When a surgeon discovers a new operating technique, when a physician discovers a new drug, when an engineer discovers a new way to harness power, all is the work of the Spirit. A famous scientist has described the way in which great discoveries are often made. A thinker thinks and thinks his way to a certain position which is just short of discovery, and there he comes to a halt, and the mind will go no further. He may remain at that mile-stone for many days and even many years, and then quite suddenly, and perhaps quite unexpectedly, the longed for solution flashes into his mind. It does not come by a process of thought; it comes by a flash of illumination. That is the work of the Holy Spirit. This is not to say the truth comes to a man who does nothing, to a man who does not work and who engages in no thought; but it is to say that, if a man uses his mind and his skill and his brain to the uttermost, the Spirit of truth comes to meet that seeking in a moment of revelation. It will also mean that many a time the Holy Spirit uses a man who does not know that he is being used, but who is nonetheless single-minded in his search for truth, and in his toil for that which will lessen the toil and alleviate the pain of men. The help of the Spirit is not the monopoly of the theologian. Truth is a many-sided thing, and in every sphere of truth the Spirit of God is He who brings God's truth to men.

(b) The Spirit is the *intermediary* of Jesus Christ and of God. The Spirit speaks to men what He hears from God (16¹³). The Spirit takes of the things of Christ and shows them unto men (16¹⁴). Here is the very way in which the Fourth Gospel was written. It was the last of the Gospels to be set down; it was not written until about A.D. 100, and the John who wrote it was a very old man. Most likely it was all of seventy years since he had companied with Jesus in the flesh on the roads of Galilee. There is more than one account in the early writers of how the Gospel came to be written. Clement of Alexandria tells us: 'Last of all, John, perceiving that the bodily facts had been made plain in the Gospel, being urged by his friends, composed a spiritual Gospel.' There is a document called the Muratorian Canon, which dates to about A.D. 170, and which contains the first official list of the books of the Church, with a brief word or two about them. It has a description of how the Fourth Gospel was written. The description is not history; it is legend. In some of the facts it cannot be accurate, for Andrew could not have been alive when the Fourth Gospel

was written, but it may well be right in its general description
of the situation. It tells its story like this: 'At the request of
his fellow-disciples and of his bishops, John, one of the
disciples said: "Fast with me for three days from this time,
and whatsoever shall be revealed to each of us, whether it be
favourable to my writing or not, let us relate it to one another."
On the same night it was revealed to Andrew that John should
relate all things, aided by the revision of all.'

Here is a flood of light on the Fourth Gospel and on the
whole transmission and interpretation of Christian truth. We
must often have wondered if the long speeches in the Fourth
Gospel were actually and verbatim and in so many words
delivered by Jesus. They are so unlike the short, pithy,
epigrammatic sayings in the first three Gospels. How can we
look for a verbatim report of these words seventy years after
they were spoken? But if we put together the work of the
Spirit in taking the things of Christ and showing them to men,
and the story in the Muratorian Canon, we arrive at a situation
something like this. John was old and his days were num-
bered. There were those who thought that before he died he
should write down his memories of Jesus. John said to those
who had also heard the Lord: 'Come, and let us pray, and let
us ask for the Spirit and let us talk together.' So they talked
reverently and long. And one would say, 'You remember that
He said . . .'. And straightway another would add, 'Yes, and
we know that He meant . . .'. And so not only the words of
Jesus, but the meaning and the significance of the words were
handed down.

The Fourth Gospel is the Gospel of the Holy Spirit. It is
the Gospel that the Holy Spirit wrote through the hand of
John. It is the Gospel of a man who under the guidance of
the Spirit had thought about Jesus Christ for seventy years
and more. In the Fourth Gospel we see the Spirit—even as
Jesus had promised—taking the things that are His and
showing them unto men.

This is precisely why the truth of the New Testament is
infinite; and this is precisely why the teacher and the preacher

need never be afraid that there is nothing left to say. Here in the Gospels we have the record of what Jesus said. But Jesus is not some one who once spoke and is now silent. Jesus is not a memory, but a presence. As someone has put it: 'No apostle ever *remembered* Jesus.' They did not *remember* Him; they *experienced* Him. And if we go to the written words of Jesus in the help of the Spirit, then still the Spirit takes of the things of Jesus Christ and shows them unto us, and new peaks and vistas of truth are for ever appearing out of the unchanging words.

(c) This leads us directly to another truth. The Holy Spirit is the *unfolder* of truth. Jesus said: 'I have yet many things to say unto you, but you cannot bear them now. Howbeit, when He the Spirit of truth is come, He will guide you into all truth' (John 16$^{12-13}$). Here is one of the most important texts in all Scripture. It means that truth can never be static; truth must always be dynamic and expanding. It is only possible to tell a man as much as he can understand and assimilate. As the Latin tag has it: '*Quicquid recipitur, recipitur ad modum recipientis*'—Whatever is received, is received in proportion as the receiver can receive it. It is not the truth which changes; it is our grasp of it which changes. We often speak of a developing revelation; we should do better to speak of a developing apprehension of God's revelation. Westcott puts it this way: 'The revelation of Christ in His person and work was absolute and complete, but without the gradual illumination of the Spirit is partly unintelligible and unobserved.'

Here there is warning. There is warning to the arrogance which believes that it has grasped the whole truth, and that there is nothing left to learn. There is warning to the intolerance which believes that it alone has the truth, and that any other interpretation of the truth must be either the error of ignorance or the heresy of malignity. Above all, there is warning to the rigidity which makes of dogma a fetter. G. H. C. Macgregor says of this passage: 'Our Gospel registers an eternal protest against all fixity of dogma.' And he relates a story of a saying of Epictetus. To a young, would-be philosopher Epictetus said warningly: 'Sir, consider, if you can bear it.'

To the Christian thinker there is open the glorious adventure of following the guidance of the Holy Spirit. All life is an unfolding. Love is not the same thing to the infant in his mother's arms, the young child, the teen-ager, the newly married couple, those who have gone down the road of the years past many milestones together, the one who is left when the other has gone from this earth. No truth is static, least of all God's truth. If we believe in the Holy Spirit, we shall be saved from intolerance, from arrogance, and from servitude to the dogmas of men.

(d) The Holy Spirit is Jesus Christ's *remembrancer*. 'The Holy Spirit', says Jesus, 'will bring all things to your remembrance, whatsoever I have said unto you' (14[26]). When we are in danger of forgetting the words of Jesus, when we sorely need to remember them, the Holy Spirit brings them back to our memory. This can operate in at least three spheres in life.

First, the Holy Spirit is *the strong ally of conscience*. It may be that some of us have more than once had the experience that, when we were in danger of falling to a temptation, some word of Scripture, some verse of a hymn, some memory of a loved one, came flashing unbidden into our minds and saved us from shame. That is the work of the Holy Spirit. The Holy Spirit reminds men of the voice of Jesus when they are in danger of forgetting it.

Secondly, the Holy Spirit is *the deep source of comfort*. It may be that in the hour of sorrow and of loss we seem to live in a world in which there is no light left, and in which there is no anaesthetic for the wound upon the heart. At such a time there may flash into our minds one of the great comforting sayings of Scripture, and suddenly the tempest becomes a calm, and the dark becomes light. As G. H. C. Macgregor puts it: 'Echoes will be reawakened, and a fuller meaning given to old truth.' The Holy Spirit brings us light in the dark, peace in the storm, comfort in tears, by reminding us of the words of Jesus Christ.

Thirdly, the Holy Spirit is *the insistent bearer of challenge*. It is easy to become lazy, lethargic, inert, complacent; it is easy to forget the tasks which cry out to be done and the duties which demand to be faced. At such a time the Holy Spirit reawakens the life which would like to drowse in a land where it is always afternoon, and confronts us with some word of Jesus which is a rallying-call to action and a challenge to new effort and new toil.

There are times in life when we need nothing so much as to be reminded of some word of Jesus, and at such times the Holy Spirit is His remembrancer.

(*e*) The Holy Spirit brings *guidance for the future*. 'He will show you things to come' (16¹³). He will show you, as some one has translated it, 'things which are on the way'. This does not mean that the Holy Spirit will write history in advance for us; it does not mean that the Holy Spirit enables us to foretell definite events and happenings, and to date them in advance. But it does mean that the Holy Spirit enables men to see the consequences ahead of any course of action that they may be taking. G. H. C. Macgregor quotes a passage from Percy Gardner's *Ephesian Gospel*: 'Through all history the prophets who have tried to detail future history have failed; but the great ones among them, who have seen into the heart of things and declared in what direction they were moving, have succeeded. The truth of prophecy is not truth to fact, but truth to idea.' The Holy Spirit can tell men what courses of action lead to the fulfilment of the will of God, and what courses of action can lead to nothing other than disaster. That is why no Church and no nation can ever prosper without men who are men of the Spirit. He who is guided by the expediency of the moment, he who is driven by the dream of national greatness or of personal prestige, he who assesses things on purely prudential motives, must in the end ruin a Church and wreck a nation. The true leader is the man of the Spirit, the man who through the Spirit sees the consequence of actions as God sees them, and who take every decision in time in the light of eternity.

(5) The Holy Spirit has *a witnessing, a convincing, and a convicting* work. 'He shall testify of me,' said Jesus (John 15²⁶). The most important passage for this is 16⁸⁻¹¹, and it is a difficult passage, partly because it is so highly compressed, and partly because the key word in it is a Greek word which can be used for more than one English word. The passage runs:

And when He [the Comforter, the Holy Spirit] is come, He will reprove the world of sin, and of righteousness, and of judgement; of sin, because they believe not on me; of righteousness, because I go to my Father, and ye see me no more; of judgement, because the prince of this world is judged.

Here the work of the Holy Spirit, to use the language of the Authorized Version, is a *reproving work*. The word for to reprove is *elegchein*. The basic meaning of this word is so to demonstrate the truth to a man that he sees it as the truth, that he is convinced of, and admits, his error, and that he accepts the new consequences which follow from the new acceptance of the truth. This may be done by argument, by cross-examination and by questioning, by confronting him with some undeniable fact, by producing witnesses who will testify to the truth. It can thus be seen that *elegchein* in Greek represents two very similar words in English. It means both *to convince* and *to convict*. *Elegchein* means both to convict a man of his fault and to convince him of his error. The whole essence of the word is that the truth is so presented to a man that he cannot fail to see it, that he cannot deny it, and that he must accept it.

In this passage we must use both meanings of *elegchein*. Let us take the three functions of the Spirit here set forth.

First, the Spirit will convict the world of sin, because they believe not on me. That is to say, the work of the Holy Spirit will compel a man to see that not to believe in Jesus Christ is to sin; the Spirit convicts a man of his sin in disregarding and disobeying Jesus Christ. As we read on through the New Testament it is not long before we see that work of the Spirit powerfully in action. After Peter's first sermon on the day of Pentecost, his hearers were pricked to the heart and asked what they must do (Acts 2³⁷). That was the work of the Holy Spirit. Why should a man be sorry for sin? If he can escape the consequences, why should he not be pleased shrewdly and cunningly to do as he likes? Whence comes the sense of sin? What wakens the sense of sin, the feeling of guilt, the sense of self-revulsion all of a sudden in a man's heart? Why should he not comfortably go on doing as he is doing, and what is it that suddenly pulls him up in horror at himself? That is the work of the Holy Spirit within his heart.

Second, the Spirit will convince of righteousness, because Jesus goes to His Father. The righteousness in question here is the righteousness of Jesus. The Holy Spirit is He who convinces a man of the supreme righteousness and the supreme greatness of Jesus Christ. Again, it is not long before we see this convincing work of the Spirit powerfully in operation. As Jesus died upon the Cross, the centurion who was in charge of the crucifixion was on his knees, breathing out in staggered amazement: 'Truly this man was the Son of God' (Matthew 27⁵⁴; Mark 15³⁹; Luke 23⁴⁷). That was the work of the Holy Spirit. How is it that anyone can see in this crucified Galilaean the Son of God? How is it that anyone can see in this penniless wandering, homeless Galilaean eccentric the supreme guide for life and for death? What is it that convinces men of the unique claims of Jesus Christ? That is the work of the Holy Spirit. This convincing is further affirmed and guaranteed, 'because', as Jesus says, 'I go to my Father, and ye see me no more.' That is to say, the supreme proof that the claims of Jesus are justified, the supreme proof that Jesus is who and what He claims to be, lies in the Resurrection and in the Ascension. Without them it might be possible to see in Jesus a glorious failure; with them we cannot but see the triumphant, victorious, vindicated Lord.

Third, The Spirit will convince men of judgement. The

Spirit will convince men that they cannot do what they like and escape the consequences. The Spirit will convince men that at the end a man stands before the judge of all the earth. Once again, it was not long before that work of the Spirit was powerfully operative. Confronted with the claims of Christ, the Philippian gaoler revealed it in his aghast question: 'Sirs, what must I do to be saved?' (Acts 16[30]). A man may look at this world and may come to the wishful conclusion that goodness has no reward and sin has no punishment. What, then, suddenly fills him with holy terror, with the realization that the new world will redress the balance of the old, that there is a God whom one day he must meet? That is the work of the Holy Spirit. It is the work of the Spirit which convinces a man that the prince of this world is ultimately defeated, that judgement in the end lies with God, and that he will face that judgement.

Here, then, is the tremendous work of the Spirit. The Spirit convinces a man of his own sin; the Spirit convinces a man of the unique perfection of Jesus Christ; the Spirit convinces a man that in the end he must meet God. There remains one thing that John did not say; we have to wait for Paul, as we shall see, to say it, although doubtless John knew it well. If the Spirit convinces a man of sin and of judgement and of the holiness of Christ, what is it that saves him from being driven to bleak despair by such a series of soul-shaking discoveries? What is it that gives him the assurance, when he sees the Cross of Christ, that in the work of Christ there is his redemption from sin? What is it that makes him as sure of salvation as he was of judgement? That, too, is the work of the Holy Spirit. The beginning, the middle and the end of the soul's surrender to Christ are the work of the Spirit. The awakening to sin, the realization of judgement, the discovery of Christ, the assurance of salvation, are all the work of the Holy Spirit of God.

CHAPTER FOUR

The Holy Spirit in the Expanding Church

THE FULL title of the book of Acts is The Acts of the Apostles. That title could equally well read The Acts of the Holy Spirit. In the early chapters of Acts no great figure in the Church either spoke or acted or came to any decision other than under the guidance of the Holy Spirit. The Holy Spirit is the principal actor in the drama of the expanding Church. That is why the first two chapters of the Book of Acts are of paramount importance for the study of the Holy Spirit. It is these two chapters which tell of the preparation for the Spirit, and of His actual coming.

Let us, then, look first at the first chapter of Acts, which tells of the preparation for the coming of the Spirit.

(1) The disciples received from Jesus *a command to wait*. They were not to leave Jerusalem and to set out on their great task at once; they were to wait for the promise of the Father (1⁴); they were to wait for the coming of the Spirit. It is as if Jesus Christ said to His men and to His Church: 'You cannot do my work without my Spirit.' We live in an age when men must always be doing something; we live in an age which believes in action. We find it very difficult to believe that time spent in waiting is not wasted time. But the fact remains that in life there can never be a foreground of effective activity without a background of passive receptivity. The supreme example of waiting is Jesus Himself. He was thirty years old before He left the retirement of Nazareth for the ministry for which He came into the world. It is quite possible for a man and for an organization and for a Church to make every possible preparation for some scheme or some undertaking except the one essential preparation—the preparation of waiting for the Spirit.

(2) The disciples received from Jesus *a promise of power*. Very soon they were to be baptized, not with water as in the baptism of John, but with the Spirit (1⁵), and when that happened they would receive power (1⁸). The word for power here used is *dunamis*. With the coming of the Spirit there would come upon them an explosive and a dynamic power. The tragedy of so much of our activity is that it is ineffective. Every one knows what it feels like to live so crowded a life that one has scarcely a moment to spare, and yet at the end of the day to have nothing to show for it. Activity without the Spirit is futile activity. The Spirit is the source, not of restless business, but of power.

(3) So, then, the disciples had received a command to wait and a promise of power; and they proceeded to wait in such a way as to give the promise every chance to come true.

They waited *with prayer and supplication* (1¹⁴). It has been said that the Christian life is in essence 'a conversation with God.' It is surely obvious that God cannot speak to us unless by listening we give Him a chance to speak. God cannot give us His gifts, especially the gift of His Spirit, unless we open ourselves to these gifts. That is what real prayer does; but it must be remembered that the prayer which finds God is one of the most strenuous activities which the spirit of man can undertake. Albert Edward Day, in his book *Existence under God*, describes this true prayer: 'It is not merely a flash of Godward desire, but the passionate fervour of a whole self that pants to know God and His will above all other knowing. It is not a hurried visit to the window of a religious drive-in restaurant for a moral sandwich or a cup of spiritual stimulant, but an unhurried communion with God who is never in a hurry. It is not merely the expression of a transient mood of dependence or loneliness, but the consistent cry of one who seeks to perceive and express the Ultimate Beauty. It is the antithesis of dilly-dally devotions, drowsy murmurs from a pillow where sleep lies in wait, the lazy lisping of familiar phrases that should shake one to the core of one's being. It is the find-or-die outreach of the soul for God.' If our reaction to the experience of the disciples is to say, 'I do not experience the Holy Spirit out of my prayers', then it may be that we should do well to ask ourselves if our prayers are 'the find-or-die outreach of the soul for God'.

(4) The disciples waited *in the right place*. They waited in an upper room (1^{13}), and surely it is safe to believe that the upper room in which they waited was the upper room in which they had companied with their Lord at the last meal together, and in which His risen presence had come to them.

It is a fact of experience that we are much more likely to be aware of God in some places than in others. When life for Jacob fell in, when his sons' conduct had made his name to stink among the inhabitants of the land, when strange gods and the strange ways had invaded his own household, and when Jacob wanted God as he had seldom wanted God before, he said: 'Let us arise and go up to Bethel' (Genesis 34^{25}–35^3). It was at Bethel that he had seen the ladder from earth to heaven and had made intimate and unmistakable contact with God (Genesis 28^{10-19}), and, when he wanted God again, it was to Bethel he returned. There is a legend about Zacchaeus. It is told that, in the days after he had met Jesus, he sometimes used to slip away alone, and no one knew where he went. One day someone followed him. Zacchaeus walked out from Jericho until he came to a certain tree by the side of the road, and he stood beside the tree touching it with a kind of caress. The one who had followed came up and said: 'Why do you stand beneath that tree, Zacchaeus, and touch it like that?' 'Because', answered Zacchaeus, 'it was from that tree that first I saw my Lord, and when I specially need to meet Him again, I come back.'

This is not to deny that a man can meet God in the open spaces on the moors, or on the hilltop, or by the sea, or in his own house and home, or on the busy streets of men; but it is to say that the Spirit of God is likeliest of all to come upon a man in the house of God, which has been hallowed by the presence of God, and in which so many have sought and found their Lord. To take a very simple human analogy, we do not ever altogether forget those whom we have loved and who have gone from us, but nonetheless there are certain places in which their presence is almost unbearably close, because once we companied with them there.

(5) The disciples waited *in fellowship*. They continued *with one accord* in prayer and supplication (1^{14}). On the Day of Pentecost they were in one place *with one accord* (2^1). There is no barrier to the coming of the Spirit like human discord. No Church which is rent by dissension, no congregation whose members are at variance with one another, no gathering in which there is division between leader and people, can ever become the home of the Spirit. The spirit of hatred necessarily shrivels the blossoming of the Spirit of the God whose name is love. 'Where love is, God is,' as Tolstoi said long ago. We should realize the reason for so many of our failures in the work of Christ, if we remembered that where there are broken personal relationships the Spirit cannot come.

(6) The disciples waited *in study of the Scriptures*. It was in the light of Scripture that they looked at the treachery of Judas and proceeded to fill his place in the apostolic company (1^{16-20}). When we read the word of God, the Spirit does not shine only *on* the page we read; the Spirit shines also *from* the page we read. In prayer and in meditation on God's word, in uninterrupted fellowship in the place hallowed by the presence of Jesus Christ, the disciples waited for the Spirit and the Spirit came.

The coming of the Spirit was at Pentecost, and Pentecost is, therefore, one of the great dates in the spiritual history of mankind. First, then, let us see when this great event happened.

The word Pentecost means *the fiftieth*, and Pentecost was so called because it fell on the fiftieth day after the Sabbath of the Passover (Leviticus 23^{15-16}). An alternative name for it was The Feast of Weeks, because it fell a week of weeks after the Passover time (Exodus 34^{22}; Deuteronomy 16^{9-10}). Since the Passover fell in the middle of April, this means that Pentecost fell early in June. It was one of the three great obligatory and compulsory feasts of the Jews, and since in

early June the weather was more favourable to travel than in
April, even more Jews came from a distance to the Feast of
Pentecost than came to the Passover. This explains the
tremendous roll-call of countries and provinces from which
the Jews came (2⁹⁻¹¹).

Like all Jewish feasts, Pentecost had two significances. It
had an *agricultural* significance. It marked the beginning of
the wheat harvest, and one of its great dramatic ceremonies
was the offering of two loaves made from the flour of the new
wheat (Leviticus 23¹⁶⁻¹⁷). Unlike the Passover bread, these
loaves were ordinary leavened bread. This was the only
sacrifice ever made in the Temple which included leaven. No
doubt the ceremony was a thanksgiving to God for ordinary
daily bread. It may well be that in the coming of the Spirit at
the time of Pentecost, when men were thanking God for their
daily bread, there is a hint that man cannot live by bread
alone, and that there are things of the spirit of man which
only the Spirit of God can satisfy.

It also had an *historical* significance. Pentecost commemor-
ated the giving of the Law on Mount Sinai. The fifty days
between the Passover and Pentecost were said to represent the
time when the bridegroom Israel was wooing the bride Torah,
or the law, so that Israel and the Law might be for ever wedded
in the sight of God. It was held that the Law was given in
seventy different languages, for there were seventy different
nations in the world, and the Law was meant for every nation.
This may well have had some effect on the idea that the
apostles were able to deliver the message of the Gospel in
different tongues so that men from every nation could understand. In later times—and there would be devout Jews who
followed some such practice even in New Testament times—
a selection was made including passages from all the five books
of the Law, and this selection was devoutly and reverently and
prayerfully read through on the evening before the feast. It
was, indeed, common for devout Jews to spend the whole
night before Pentecost awake in the study of the Law. It is
by no means impossible that the apostles themselves did that,

before the coming of the Spirit. One other fact remains to be added. It was the law that on Pentecost no servile work was to be done, and therefore Pentecost was a day of holiday and rest for all servants and for all slaves. It can be seen that Pentecost was a fitting date for the coming of the Spirit; the very preparations which a man would take to keep the Feast of Pentecost were preparations which would fit him and make him receptive for the coming of the Spirit.

We have more than once used the phrase 'the coming of the Spirit,' and we have already seen that John (7³⁹) makes the startling statement that during Jesus' life in the flesh the Spirit had not yet come, because Jesus had not yet been glorified. Such words do not at all deny the eternal existence of the Holy Spirit. It has often happened that although a thing has for long existed, yet men have entered into possession of enjoyment of it at some definite time. To take an obvious example, atomic power has always existed; the twentieth century did not invent it; it has always existed in the very structure of the world. But it was not until the twentieth century that men were able to tap the resources of atomic power, and so to use it and to some extent to possess it. Similarly, the Spirit had always existed with God; but it was not until Pentecost that the floodgates were opened and the tides of the Spirit flowed in among men. Pentecost was the realization and the appropriation by men of a power and a presence which were always there.

Let us, then, turn to the events of Pentecost.

(1) Something happened at Pentecost, but what happened is not reducible to words. All that Luke can do, as he tells the story, is to use analogies and pictures. There was a sound *as of* a mighty rushing wind (2²); there appeared tongues *like as* of fire (2³). There must be no crude literalism here, for Luke is seeking to describe the indescribable and to express the inexpressible. All we can say is that a power and a presence like the strength of wind and the purifying of fire came upon them. It is never possible to reduce the experience of divine action to human words.

(2) Out of this experience the disciples entered into *a new-found courage*. With utter fearlessness Peter addressed the crowd, and boldly proclaimed the message of the gospel. Here, indeed, is a complete revolution. Nothing is clearer than the complete collapse of the disciples after the arrest of Jesus. They all forsook Him and fled (Matthew 26[56]; Mark 14[50]). It was then that Peter sunk to the great denial in whose craven hour he denied all knowledge of Jesus (Matthew 26[69-75]; Mark 14[66-72]; Luke 22[54-62]; John 18[15, 18, 25-7]). When the disciples met again in the Upper Room, the doors were locked for fear of the Jews and they trembled at every step on the stair (John 20[19]). There was a time when they believed that all there was to do was to go back to the boats and to forget. 'I go afishing,' said Peter (John 21[3]). There was nothing to do but to try to take up the threads of life again, and to forget.

But now there is a revolution. That process of rehabilitation was begun by the Resurrection and completed by Pentecost. It was Voltaire who said of God that, 'If God did not exist, it would have been necessary to invent Him'. If we did not know that the Resurrection had taken place, and if we did not know that there had been a time of Pentecost, it would have been necessary to invent them to explain the change in the disciples from terror to heroism, and to explain the very existence of the Christian Church.

The first effect of Pentecost was to fill the disciples with a courage which could face the world undaunted and unafraid, glorying in the message of the gospel.

(2) Out of this experience of Pentecost the disciples gained *a new-found message*. In Acts 2 in the words of Peter we have the first sermon of the Christian Church; and it is no affair of guessing and groping and struggling for words; it is a complete and highly intelligible whole. As it stands, it has four elements in it. (i) The great days which the prophets promised and dreamed of have come, and the new age has dawned (Acts 2[16-21]). Men are living in a new creation. (ii) The new age has come through this very same Jesus who was crucified,

resurrected and exalted (2^{22-35}). The agent of this new creation, the introducer of this new age is this very same Jesus of Nazareth. (iii) This Jesus is the Messiah, the Anointed One of God, and is now exalted to the right hand of God (2^{36}). He whom they regarded as a criminal, He whom they drove to a cross, He whom they sought to eliminate, is none other than the divine and royal Son of God. (iv) Since these things are so, men are summoned to repent, to be baptized, to be forgiven, and to receive the Spirit (2^{38}).

Here is the first Christian sermon, and the amazing thing about it is that in it there is the whole of Christian theology in a nutshell, the quintessence of the Christian faith. Here is the message given by the Spirit to men.

(3) Out of this experience of Pentecost there came to the disciples *a new insight into Scripture*. If ever the Jews were to be convinced of the claims of Christ, they would have to be convinced out of their own Scriptures. They would have to be compelled to see that it was to none other than Jesus of Nazareth that all the Scriptures and all the prophets pointed. And the significant thing about the preaching of Peter is that its every statement is based on Jewish Scripture (2^{16-21}, $^{25-8}$, $^{34-5}$). The Holy Spirit enabled the disciples to see in Scripture meanings, significances, pointers, that they had never seen before. Only the Spirit can interpret the Scripture which the Spirit has inspired.

(4) Out of this experience of Pentecost there came to the disciples *the power to communicate their message*. Here we come to the most difficult problem in interpretation in this passage. We read that, when the disciples were filled with the Holy Spirit, they 'began to speak with other tongues, as the Spirit gave them utterance' (2^4). There are three possible interpretations of that passage.

(*a*) It could mean that the disciples spoke in foreign languages. Two facts make that unlikely. First, it was unnecessary. In the long list of countries given in verses 9-11 it is not meant that there were Gentile foreigners from these countries present in Jerusalem, but that there were Jews of the Dispersion from these countries who had come up to the Holy City to keep the Feast of Pentecost. In that case only two languages were necessary to make the message intelligible to all—Aramaic and Greek. It would in fact be true, except in the most remote areas, that a man speaking Greek would be understood anywhere in the Mediterranean world. In those days everyone who lived within touch of civilization spoke two languages—his own language and Greek, which was the universal language of trade and commerce, the *lingua franca* of the ancient world. In a world where Greek and Aramaic would serve all necessary purposes, a miracle whereby the disciples spoke in foreign languages was unnecessary. Second, if this was a gift made to the disciples at the time of Pentecost, it was one which did not last, for the power to speak foreign languages untaught was certainly something that the early missionaries did not possess. For two reasons, therefore, it seems unlikely that we should take the words 'other tongues' to mean 'foreign tongues'.

(b) It could mean that the disciples 'spoke with tongues'. Speaking with tongues is a phenomenon which has always been, and still is, present in the Christian Church. It is the pouring forth of a flood and torrent of sounds in no known language, sounds which are quite unintelligible unless there is some one present with the gift of interpreting them. This was a phenomenon which flourished in the early Church. Paul deals with it in 1 Corinthians 14, for it was a feature of the life of the Church in Corinth. Paul did not deny that it was a spiritual gift, but he rather deprecated its use because of its unintelligibility (1 Corinthians 14[19]), and because anyone entering a gathering in which this speaking with tongues was going on would think that he had entered an assembly of madmen (1 Corinthians 14[23]). The one point in favour of this interpretation of the Pentecost narrative is that there were those in the crowd in Jerusalem who thought that the disciples were drunk with new wine (Acts 2[13, 15]), for certainly a man speaking with tongues might well seem to be speaking drunken gibberish. But the point which finally decides against this interpretation is that quite certainly the crowd understood what the disciples were saying and were deeply affected by it.

(c) The third interpretation is that this is a vivid and dramatic way of saying that the disciples were empowered by the Spirit to speak the message of the gospel in such a way that it found a road straight to the heart of men and women of every origin and of every background. This, we think, is the true explanation of this passage. Certainly the meaning is that the disciples spoke the truth of Christ in such a way that it struck home to every heart.

Here, then, was the effect of the coming of the Spirit upon the disciples. The Spirit gave them a courage which wiped out the last remnants of fear; the Spirit gave them a message which had the quintessential truth in it; the Spirit illuminated Scripture for them, until all Scripture spoke of Jesus Christ; the Spirit opened for them a door of utterance, and gave them the power to communicate that which they had received.

Let us now turn to the rest of the narrative of the Book of Acts. Acts begins with the story of the coming of the Spirit, and goes on to show us a Church which was dominated by the Spirit.

In the thought of Acts the Spirit has always been active and operative amongst men. David spoke in the Spirit (1^{16}, 4^{25}) and so did Isaiah (28^{25}). The Spirit has always been the messenger of God's truth and God's guidance to men.

All the great figures in Acts are men of the Spirit. Filled with the Spirit, Peter addressed the Sanhedrin (4^8). When there was need of new workers within the Church, the instruction was to seek out seven men of honest report and full of the Spirit (6^3). Stephen was full of faith and of the Holy Spirit (6^5), and it was that fact which enabled him to look up and to see the glory of God and the exalted Christ as he died a martyr's death (7^{55}). Paul was filled with the Holy Spirit at the beginning of his ministry for Christ (9^{17}, 13^8). Barnabas was a good man, full of the Holy Spirit and of faith (11^{24}). The criterion by which the early Church judged a man was his relationship to the Holy Spirit. The only leaders who could lead for Christ were men who were men of the Spirit. It is even said of Jesus Himself that God anointed Him with the Holy Spirit and with power (10^{38}).

One of the unmistakable features of Acts is the way in which it tells us that every great decision which the Church took was taken under the guidance of the Spirit. It is the Holy Spirit who tells Philip to approach the Ethiopian in his chariot (8^{29}). It is the Spirit who tells Peter that men from Cornelius await him, and who bids him to go with them nothing doubting (10^{19}, 11^{12}). It is the Spirit who tells the prophets and teachers of Antioch to set apart Paul and Barnabas for the mission to the Gentiles (13^2), and it is by the Holy Spirit that these two are sent out (13^4). It is the Spirit who guides and directs the decisions of the Council of Jerusalem, whereby the Gentiles are welcomed into the Christian Church (15^{28-9}).

The significant fact is that every one of these references to the Spirit is a reference to an occasion on which a decision was taken to bring the gospel to the Gentiles. It was the Spirit who made the Church a missionary Church; it was the Spirit who enabled the Jewish leaders of the Church to forget Jewish intolerance and Jewish particularism and Jewish exclusiveness. It was the Spirit who enabled the Jewish leaders of the Church to see that Israel was chosen for a light to the Gentiles. The plain fact we see in Acts is that, had it not been for the guidance of the Spirit, the Church might well have remained nothing more than a sect of Judaism, and we should not have known the precious things of the gospel today.

In particular, we see the Spirit guiding and directing the life and activity of Paul. It is by the Spirit that he is directed away from Asia and Bithynia (16^{6-7}), and that he comes to Europe with the story of Jesus. It is in the Spirit that he passes through Macedonia (19^{21}), and that he goes to Jerusalem (20^{22}).

It is the Spirit who gives the people of the early Church information and guidance in definite situations. It is through the Spirit that Jesus gave His commandments to the waiting apostles (1^2). It is through the Spirit that Agabus foretells the famine which is to come upon the East (11²⁸). It is the Spirit who tells Paul that imprisonment and suffering await him in Jerusalem (20²³, 21⁴).

The early Church in the days of Acts had a tremendous consciousness of being divinely led. It was not that they stifled or obliterated their human minds and intellects; but that after they had brought all the powers of thought and vision and discussion and debate to bear upon any subject or any decision, their final action was always to submit the whole matter to the verdict of the Holy Spirit. It was not that the Holy Spirit was a substitute for careful thought; it was not that the Holy Spirit absolved a man from the duty of thinking and planning. It was that the leaders of the early Church were for ever conscious that they were never left to take their decisions alone. We might well be saved from many an error and a mistake, if we began and ended all our plans by waiting for the guidance of the Holy Spirit.

It was the Holy Spirit who gave a man his office in the Church. Paul reminded the Ephesian elders that it was the Holy Spirit who had made them overseers of the flock of Christ (20²⁸). Many an officer-bearer might well take his office more seriously, and perform it more diligently, if he remembered that his responsibility was not to any congregation, and not to any minister, but to none other than the Holy Spirit.

As Acts sees it, the mark of a Church is the presence of the Spirit. The Churches of Judaea walked in the fear of the Lord and in the comfort of the Holy Spirit (9³¹). In Antioch the disciples were filled with joy and the Holy Spirit (13⁵²). The reality of Christian experience was demonstrated and guaranteed by the gift of the Spirit (10⁴⁵, 15⁸). The real test of a Church lies not in the statistics which an ecclesiastical year-book can convey, but in the presence or absence of the Spirit.

In Acts the Holy Spirit is connected with certain actions and with certain people.

The Holy Spirit is connected with *prayer*. It was when the Christians had prayed, that the place was shaken and they were filled with the Holy Spirit (4^{31}). Peter and John prayed for the Samaritans, that they might receive the Holy Spirit (8^{15}). It is the man of prayer who receives the Spirit.

The Holy Spirit is connected with *preaching*. It was while Peter was preaching to Cornelius and his people that the Holy Spirit fell on all who heard the word (10^{44}, 11^{15}). The Holy Spirit comes to those who listen to, and who study, God's word.

The Holy Spirit is connected with *fasting*. It was while the prophets and teachers of Antioch were ministering and fasting that the Holy Spirit told them to separate Paul and Barnabas for the mission to the Gentiles (13^2). The Holy Spirit comes to the man who leads a disciplined life of devotion.

The Holy Spirit, in a very special way, is connected with *baptism*. It must be remembered that the narrative of Acts comes from a time before the emergence of the Christian family, and before there was anything like a Christianized society. It comes from the time when every man who came into the Church came direct from paganism and came with a perfectly deliberate act of decision. For these reasons baptism in the time of Acts was different from what it is for many of us. Baptism was an act connected with Christian witness, confession of faith, and deliberate and spontaneous entry into the fellowship of the Church. Baptism was, therefore, necessarily *adult* baptism and *instructed* baptism. A man heard the message of Jesus Christ, was touched by it, was instructed in it, determined to give his allegiance to it, and was thus baptized. Sometimes we read that it was impossible to refuse baptism because already the Holy Spirit had come; sometimes we read that the coming of the Spirit was the consequence of baptism (10^{45}, 19^{5-6}). Baptism was a time of the coming of the Spirit. In the moment when a man volunteered upon the service of Christ, the Spirit came upon him to give him strength and guidance for the task to which he had put his hand, and for the way on which he had set out.

Very closely associated with this is the fact that in Acts the Spirit is closely connected with *the laying on of hands* by apostolic men. After Philip's mission to the Samaritans, Peter and John went down to Samaria and laid their hands on them and they received the Holy Spirit (8^{15-18}). After his conversion there came to Paul his sight and the gift of the Holy Spirit when Ananias laid his hands upon him (9^{17}).

It is necessary that we should understand the significance of this, lest we think of this laying on of hands, and of this coming of the Spirit as a purely mechanical thing. In Jewish thought the laying on of hands was used in three connections. It was used for *the transference of guilt*. On the Day of Atonement the High Priest laid his hands upon the scapegoat, and so transferred to the goat the sins of the people, and the goat bore them away into the desert (Leviticus 16^{21}). It was used for *the transference of blessing*. So Jacob laid his hand upon the head of Ephraim, Joseph's son (Genesis 48^{14}). It was used for *the transference of authority*. So Moses laid his hands upon the head of Joshua his successor, and by doing so put some of his honour upon him (Numbers 27^{18}). And to this it must be added that Jesus often laid His hand upon those whom He healed.

It is in light of all this that we must think of the apostles laying their hands on the new converts into Christianity that they might receive the Spirit. But this can never become a merely mechanical matter; it can never become a merely 'official' routine; it can never become a matter of 'apostolic succession' in the narrower sense of the term. The efficacy of the laying on of hands depended altogether on the spiritual authority of the man whose hands they were. In the early Church the place of the apostles was unique; they were Christ's men; they had companied with Him in the days of His flesh, and to them He had entrusted His task. They witnessed mightily for the faith; they risked their lives for it; and one by one they died a martyr's death. It was because they were spiritual giants among men that they were able to convey the Spirit to men. I remember when I was very young being taken by my father to visit a great saint of the Church in his retirement and his old age. When the time came to go, my father stopped at the door. 'If I leave the boy with you for a moment', he said to the aged saint, 'will you put your hands on his head and bless him?' So for a moment I was left with the old man, and he placed his hands on my head and blessed me, and I have not forgotten the feeling of that moment to this day more than forty years after it. It was not simply because he was an ordained minister of the Church that that old man's blessing was so vividly effective. It was because he was who he was. There is only one true apostolic succession, and that is not the succession of those who are within any Church or who have been 'ordained' in any particular way. It is the succession of those who themselves have the Spirit of Christ in every Church.

In the early Church the Spirit came at baptism and by the laying on of the hands of apostolic men, because these men themselves had the Spirit of Christ.

This gift of the Spirit is the gift of God to every man. The invitation of Peter was flung broadcast at the crowd to come and to repent and to be baptized and to receive the Spirit (2^{38}). Peter's companions were astonished that the Holy Spirit had fallen on the Gentiles too (10^{45}); and Paul and Barnabas cited the fact that God had given the Spirit to the Gentiles as the witness of God that the door of the Church must be opened to every nation (15^8). The one thing which should break all barriers down, the one thing which should make all Churches into one, is the great basic fact that all Christians, of every race and Church, are the recipients of the one Spirit.

In these early days the effects of the Spirit were so plain for all to see that Simon Magus tried to buy from Peter the power of conferring the Spirit upon others (8^{15-19}). In particular the Spirit gave to the Christian an irresistible power in his witness (5^{22}, 6^{10}), and an indestructible joy in his life (13^{52}).

There remain three passages in Acts at which we must look. In Acts 19^{15} we read of the company of men who knew nothing at all of the Holy Spirit, and to whom Paul by baptism and laying on of hands brought the gift of the Spirit. These people knew the baptism of John; they knew what it was to repent; but they did not know what it was to receive the Spirit. These people still have their spiritual descendants, people who have a vivid sense of sin, people who know what it is even bitterly to repent, but people who have never entered into the joy and the power of living in the Spirit. Without the Spirit a man may know that he is a sinner; only with the Spirit will he know that he is a forgiven sinner. Without the Spirit there can be no such thing as the joy of Christian living and the mastery over life.

In Acts 7[51] Stephen says that the Jews of his day, like their forefathers, resist the Spirit. It is the Spirit who brings God's guidance to men. As someone put it, God in giving us free will has left us 'free to be faithless.' Every gift can be refused, and the gift of the Spirit can be refused, for God has given to men the terrible responsibility of being able to go their own way.

In Acts 5[3, 9] the charge against Annas and Sapphira is that they have lied to, and tempted, the Holy Spirit in keeping back part of the price of the property which they have sold, and in failing to give it to the Church. We must read this incident in the light of the fact that in the early Church every decision of the Church was regarded as a decision of the Spirit; and, therefore, he who tried secretly and treacherously to evade the decision of the Spirit was guilty of lying to the Spirit.

There is no book in the New Testament in which the Holy Spirit becomes so personally vivid as He does in the Book of Acts. We may well find the reason for that in two incidents in the life of Paul. When Paul was up against things in Ephesus and was in danger and in trouble, the Lord spoke to him in a vision of the night, and told him not to be afraid but to speak with boldness, 'for I am with thee' (18[9-10]). When Paul was in prison in Jerusalem and things looked black, once again the Lord stood by him to assure him that, as he had borne witness in Jerusalem, so he would also bear witness in Rome (23[11]). The significant thing about these two incidents is that they tell of visits to Paul of the Risen Lord; but they might equally well have been told as visits of the Spirit. It would have meant the same thing. What gives the Spirit His personal vividness in Acts is the fact that the work of the Spirit and the presence of the Risen Lord are one and the same thing. In Acts the presence of the Spirit is the fulfilment of the promise of Christ that He would be with His own even to the end of the world (Matthew 28[20]).

CHAPTER FIVE

The Holy Spirit in the Letters of Paul

WHEN WE study the conception of the Holy Spirit in the letters of Paul, we are confronted with such a wealth of material that the orderly arrangement of it becomes a well-nigh impossible task. In this matter there is one basic difference between Paul and John. John is the man of contemplation and Paul is the man of action. That is not for a moment to say that John did not act and Paul did not think; but it is to say that John's experience of the Holy Spirit is the experience of a man who through a long life had thought and meditated and contemplated the wonder of the Spirit, while Paul's experience of the Spirit is the experience of a man who had travelled more miles and seen more countries and crowded more adventures into his life than any other man in the Christian Church. That is why Paul's teaching on the Holy Spirit must always be the study of any man who in any age embarks upon a missionary career for Jesus Christ.

In his thinking about the Holy Spirit, Paul begins where the New Testament always begins, with the fundamental fact that *the Holy Spirit is the gift of God.*

> *All good gifts around us*
> *Are sent from heaven above,*

and that is particularly true of the gift of the Spirit. Paul prays that God may give His people the Spirit (Ephesians 1[17]). He speaks of God who has given us His Holy Spirit (1 Thessalonians 4[8]). He speaks of the Holy Spirit who is given unto us (Romans 5[5]).

But on two occasions Paul uses a word with a wealth of meaning in it. In Galatians 3[5] he speaks of God *ministering* His Holy Spirit to us, and in Philippians 1[19] he speaks of the *supply* of the Spirit of Jesus Christ. In Galatians the verb is *epichorēgein*, and in Philippians the noun is the *epichorēgia*. These words are great words with a great history, and their predominant note is generosity, lavishness, abundance. The word *chorēgia* goes back to the greatest days of Athens. One of the greatest of all the glories of Athens was the plays which the great writers produced, the plays which Aeschylus and Sophocles and Euripides and Aristophanes wrote, many of which are still the cherished possessions of mankind. All these plays involved the dressing, the maintaining and the training of a chorus, for in those plays the chorus was an integral actor in the play. It was the custom for public-spirited and generous Athenian citizens to make themselves entirely responsible for all such equipment and training and maintenance, and in the case of the choruses for the dithyrambs that might involve expenses for fifty men and youths. The undertaking of such a duty was called a *chorēgia*. Clearly the undertaking of a *chorēgia* was the action of a man who loved his city and was prepared to be lavishly generous to it.

So, then, this word *chorēgia* has from the beginning loving generosity in it. But as time goes on the meaning of the word widens. It comes to be used in certain definite connections. (*a*) It is regular in marriage contracts. 'Let the husband supply (*chorēgein*) the wife with all necessaries according to his means.' It is the word for the support which a man in honour and in love was bound to give his wife. (*b*) It is regularly used of equipping an army for war. It is used of sending into battle men who are fully and generously equipped for the struggle which lies ahead of them. (*c*) It is used of a man's natural endowment for life. For instance, it is used of the physical strength and bodily fitness of a gymnast or an athlete. Aristotle uses it of the man who is furnished with virtue, and furnished with sufficient means to put that virtue into action, and who is, therefore, equipped for the leading of the happy life.

The words *chorēgia* and *chorēgein* describe the necessary provision of equipment for the successful undertaking of duty with honour and with efficiency in any walk of life. Through the Holy Spirit God equips us to play our part in the great action of the drama of life. Through the Holy Spirit God cares for us and supplies our every need, as a bridegroom does for his bride, and a husband for his wife. Through the Holy Spirit God equips and arms us for the battle and for the campaign of life, so that we may face with gallantry every assault which life makes upon us. Through the Holy Spirit God equips us for the business of life and living, as a parent would wish to see his child equipped with every natural resource. The very word Paul uses to describe God's giving of the Holy Spirit is itself an expression of the lavish generosity of God.

This Spirit comes to us through Jesus Christ. It is the Spirit of His Son that God sends to us (Galatians 4[6]). It is the supply of the Spirit of Jesus Christ that we receive (Philippians 1[19]). The Spirit is the Spirit of Christ (Ephesians 3[16]). But how then do we receive this Spirit? Is the Spirit given to everyone? Is the coming of the Spirit upon a man something with which a man has nothing to do, and something which is quite independent of what kind of a man he is? It is the insistence of Paul that we receive the Spirit through faith (Galatians 3[2, 5, 14]). Faith in Paul is always a double-sided thing. We may put it in either of two ways, both of which ultimately mean the same thing. Faith is *reception* and *action*, or faith is *trust* and *obedience*. Faith is the acceptance both of the *offer* of Christ and of the *commands* of Christ. When a man accepts the offer of Christ, and when he sets out to live in the impossible way which that offer involves and demands, then the Holy Spirit comes upon him, and the impossible becomes the possible. Christianity is always privilege and responsibility combined. So faith means the realization and the acceptance of the privilege which is offered to us and of the responsibility which is laid upon us. To accept the offer of Christ in trust and to obey the commands of Christ in obedience together form the way to the full receiving of the Spirit.

The place in the Christian life which Paul assigns to the

Holy Spirit may perhaps best be seen from two vivid and pictorial words which he uses to describe the Spirit.

Three times Paul speaks about the *earnest* of the Spirit. Twice he speaks about God who has given us the earnest of the Spirit (2 Corinthians 1²², 5⁵), and in Ephesians (1¹⁴) he speaks about the Holy Spirit who is the earnest of our inheritance. The word which Paul uses in these three cases is the word *arrabōn*. This was a regular Greek word of business and of trade. When a deal was completed, or when a contract was entered into, it was common to pay an *arrabōn*. The *arrabōn* was the first instalment of the price or of the fee, and was the token and guarantee that in due time the full payment would follow.

There are many occurrences of this word in the papyri. Copreus, a musician, agrees to bring his flute-players and his musicians to a five-day village festival; the full terms are agreed; and then there follows the acknowledgment: 'He acknowledges that he has received herewith 20 drachmae as *arrabōn*.' In a papyrus which deals with shares in a certain property, one of the parties acknowledges that he has received 14 drachmae as *arrabōn* out of the 21 drachmae which was the full price. The president of the village council of Bacchias arranges to hire a troop of castanet dancing-girls for certain village celebrations. Their pay, their maintenance and their transport are all arranged; and so much—the papyrus is mutilated and the exact figure is missing—is paid in advance as *arrabōn*. A mouse-catcher is engaged to rid a vineyard of mice, and in order that he may begin his work at once and without delay, he is paid 8 drachmae as *arrabōn*. Here we have a common Greek business word, describing a way of doing business with which everyone in the ancient world was perfectly familiar. The *arrabōn*, the earnest, was the first instalment of a promised price or fee, and it was the assurance that in due time the full price would be paid.

So when Paul speaks of the Holy Spirit as the *arrabōn* which God has given us, he means that the experience of the Holy Spirit is the first instalment of the life of heaven, that life in the Holy Spirit is the foretaste of the life everlasting and the guarantee that life everlasting is sure to follow. The strength, the light, the power, the joy, the peace, which come through the Holy Spirit are the foretaste, even in this life, of all that life in the presence of God will be. Life in the Spirit here and now is the beginning of the life everlasting. To possess the Holy Spirit and all His gifts is to know, even if it be distantly, what heaven will be like.

The second vivid picture which Paul uses is the picture of sealing with the Holy Spirit. God, he says, has *sealed* us (*sphragizein*), and given us the earnest of the Spirit (2 Corinthians 1²²). After you believed, he writes, you were sealed with the promised Holy Spirit (Ephesians 1¹³). The Christian is sealed with the Spirit to the day of redemption (Ephesians 4³⁰).

In the ancient world sealing was a very common practice, and the papyri supply us with many instances of it. A seal was used for a variety of purposes.

It was used *to guarantee safety and security*. When the military authorities left property which they wished to use again and which they wished no one else to enter, they left a seal on the door. When a book was a very sacred book, and when its contents were for none but the initiated, it was sealed in order to keep it safe.

It was used as *an attestation of truth*. A will or a deposition was always sealed by the witness to attest the fact that it was valid and true.

It was used as *a guarantee of quality*. Corn was sent in sealed sacks, wine was sent in sealed jars, and the unbroken seal was a guarantee of the genuine quality of the contents. A correspondent wrote with a gift: 'I send you a box of very excellent grapes and of excellent dates under seal.' A certain Promethion sent to Zenon '10 hins of perfume in 21 vases sealed with my finger ring'. Animals for sacrifice were carefully examined, and then, if they were found to be unblemished and fit to offer to the gods, they were duly sealed. Repeatedly the seal was the guarantee of the quality of the goods to which it is attached.

It was used as *a sign of ownership.* An agent was instructed to see that an ass was branded and sealed, so that there could be no dispute about its ownership. If a man wished to stamp something as his, he set his seal upon it, thereby affirming his ownership for all the world to see.

So, then, as Paul sees it, the Holy Spirit is God's protection on a man. The possession of the Holy Spirit is the guarantee of the reality of a man's faith. The fruit of the Spirit, the possession of the Spirit, is God's seal upon a man, the unanswerable proof that that man belongs to God. When a man is clearly living in the Spirit, when he is showing to all men a wisdom, a strength, a purity, a courage, an ability to cope with life that the ordinary man does not possess, that is the guarantee that his faith is real and genuine, and that is the mark of God's ownership of him. To be a Christian is to know the power of the Spirit. The difference between the Christian and the non-Christian lies precisely in the fact that the Christian has in his life the unmistakable fruit of the Spirit. When others waver, the Spirit gives him certainty. When others collapse, the Spirit enables him to pass the breaking-point and not to break. When others fall before their temptations and soil their garments, he is enabled to overcome temptation and to do the right and to keep himself unspotted from the world.

We have said that the Spirit is the gift of God; we have said that that gift comes through Jesus Christ; and we have seen that the Spirit is the very badge of the man of God. We can go further. The most startling thing that Paul says about the Spirit is the statement: The Lord is the Spirit (2 Corinthians 3^{17}). When Paul wrote that, he was not thinking in terms of the doctrine of the Trinity and the persons in the Godhead; he was not thinking theologically at all; he was speaking from experience, and his experience was that to possess the Spirit was nothing less than to possess Jesus Christ.

In Paul's thought and experience the Holy Spirit has a special and unique part to play in man's relationship to God.

It is through the Holy Spirit that the love of God is shed

abroad within our hearts (Romans 5⁵). For any man who is conscious of sin there is nothing more difficult to believe than that God loves him. For any man who is conscious of his own unimportance and his own worthlessness there is nothing more difficult than to believe that Jesus Christ died for him. It is the Holy Spirit who enters into sin-conscious hearts and convinces us that God does love us and that Christ did die for us.

It is through the Holy Spirit that we have access to God (Ephesians 2¹⁸). The word which Paul uses for *access* is *prosagōgē*. It may well be that the picture which was in Paul's mind was the picture of an earthly court. In the ancient world a king was hedged about by many barriers, and it was difficult, if not impossible, to gain access to his presence. Usually he had a trusted court official whose task it was to decide who was to be admitted to the king's presence and who was to be kept out. The title of that official was the *prosagōgeus*, the introducer. The Holy Spirit is God's introducer, the one who opens the door and brings us into the presence of God. That is to say, it is the Holy Spirit in our hearts who gives us the desire and the confidence to enter into the presence of God.

But there is a much closer relationship than the relationship of king and subject. It is through the Holy Spirit that we are adopted into the family of God (Romans 8¹⁴⁻¹⁶). Those who are lead by the Spirit become the children of God. It is through the Spirit that we learn to call God Father, and to know that we are His children. In the ancient world adoption was the most final of all processes. The previous parents completely abandoned all rights and claims to the child, and in the new family the child ranked as a real and genuine son, with full rights of inheritance. So complete was the process of adoption that, when a person was adopted, he was regarded as so completely changed that even all his previous debts and obligations were cancelled. It is that way with us and God. He accepts us fully into His family; our past is past and done with; we enter into the inheritance of the saints; we become children of God. Instead of fearing God, we learn to call Him

Father. Behind all this process is the Holy Spirit. It is the Holy Spirit who puts into our heart the desire to become one of the family of God; it is the Holy Spirit who assures us, as we have seen, of the love of God, and of our welcome into that new family; it is the leading of the Holy Spirit which brings us out of the possession of the world and into the possession of God.

When we enter the family of God, it is by the work of the Holy Spirit that we are sanctified (1 Corinthians 6[11]; 2 Corinthians 3[18]; 2 Thessalonians 2[13]). Clearly, when we enter into the family of God, we take upon ourselves new obligations; we enter upon a new way of life. We cannot remain as we are, and, as Fosdick put it, the glory of the Christian message is that no man need stay the way he is. We are cleansed from the impurities which soiled life; more, we are changed from glory into glory. And the agent of our sanctification is the Holy Spirit, the power of God operative within our lives.

If this is to be so, there must enter into life a new awareness of sin and a new sensitiveness to goodness. And it is the Holy Spirit who acts through conscience to show us what we ought to do and how we ought to live (Romans 9[1]). The Holy Spirit becomes the divine director of the man who has entered into the family of God.

It is the Holy Spirit who gives us the assurance of our salvation. It is because of the work of the Holy Spirit within our hearts that we know that we are within the family of God, and that we know that we can call God Father (Romans 8[16]; Galatians 4[6]). It is the influence of the Holy Spirit within our hearts which takes away our last doubts and which makes us sure that all the promises of God are true.

In view of the greatness of Paul's conception of the Spirit, it is only natural to find that in Paul's experiences the greatest gifts of the Christian life come in and through the Spirit.

Righteousness comes through the Spirit (Romans 14[17]). The word for *righteousness* is *dikaiosunē*, which in the New Testament is a word of two meanings. (*a*) It is the great Greek word to describe the essence of the good life. The Greek definition declared that this *righteousness* consisted in giving to the gods and to men that which was their due. For the Greek to be righteous was perfectly to fulfil all duties both to God and to man. (*b*) But *dikaiosunē* in Paul's writings is also the great key word of *justification by faith*. We must be careful to understand what Paul means when he uses the words *justification* and *justify*, for the meaning is not the normal English meaning of these words. When in ordinary speech we talk of justifying a person, we mean that we produce reasons to show and to prove that he is right to think or to speak or to act as he did. For us *justification* is the process of proving that a person (whether ourselves or someone else) is blameless and correct. But it is perfectly obvious this is not Paul's meaning, that by justification he does not mean the process by which we prove to God that we are right! In Greek the verb *to justify* is *dikaioun*. Greek verbs which end in *-oun* do not normally mean to make a person something; they mean to reckon, to account, to treat, to regard a person as something. Therefore, *dikaioun* means to reckon, to account, to treat, to regard a person as just, as a good person. And precisely here is the amazing wonder of justification by faith. Justification by faith means that for the sake of Jesus Christ God reckons, accounts, treats, regards us as good persons, sinners though we are. That is why Moffatt translates *dikaioun* by the English word *acquit*. But even that will not do, because according to law a person who is acquitted must be innocent, whereas in the great truth of justification by faith the person who is accepted by God as good is a literally hell-deserving sinner. Now clearly that great and precious fact creates between us and God a completely new relationship. So long as we think of God in terms of judgement and justice, then there can be nothing but fear. Montaigne once said: 'There is no man so good, who, were he to submit his thoughts and actions to the laws, would not deserve hanging ten times in his life.' If that is true of a man in regard to human law, how much more is it true of a man in regard to divine law? But through Jesus Christ the Saviour we make the tremendous discovery that God in His amazing love is willing to treat sinners, such as we are, as if they had been good persons. The moment we discover that, and the moment we stake our faith on that, we are in a new relationship with God. The estrangement, the distance, the fear, the terror, are gone, and we are intimately, lovingly, gratefully at home with God. It is that new relationship with God that the word *dikaiosunē* describes. Again and again we get the sense of *dikaiosunē* far better if we translate it *a right relationship with God*, and we get the sense of *dikaioun* far better if we translate it *to put into a right relationship with God*. To take only one example, let us apply this principle of translation to Romans 5[1]; it will then read: 'Since through faith we have been put into a right relationship with Him, we have peace with God through our Lord Jesus Christ.'

But the matter does not end there. Are we then to say that sin does not matter? Are we then to say that, since God in His wondrous love accepts the sinner as a good man, we are free to sin as we like? Far from it. To say that is to say that we are free to hurt love as much as we like. There is no compulsion like the compulsion of love. We do not say: 'So-and-so loves me, and will forgive me no matter what I do; therefore I will sin as I like.' We say: 'So-and-so loves me, and will forgive me whatever I do; therefore I must strive never to disappoint him or to grieve his heart.' To be loved is to be compelled to some kind of honour and nobility.

Now here exactly is where the two meanings of righteousness run into each other. Righteousness is a new relationship with God in which we become joyfully aware that God has not allowed our sin to separate us from Him, but has treated us as if we had not sinned at all. And that very generosity of God *compels* us, *drives* us, *inspires* us, to be righteous, to make a never-ending effort to render to God and to man what is their due. To put this in Pauline language, justification must be followed by the process of sanctification. Justification without sanctification is an empty term.

It is here that the work of the Spirit comes in. And in this the work of the Spirit is twofold. First, how can we believe that God is like this towards sinners? The good news seems far too good to be true. It is the work of the Holy Spirit in our hearts to assure us that the good news is true, and that we can stake everything on it. The Holy Spirit, if we may put it so, is the liaison officer of the good news of God. Second, we are faced with the impossible task of seeking to be worthy of this love, of being righteous in the ethical sense of the term. It is only in the daily help of the Spirit that the victory over self and sin and Satan can be won. It is only in the Spirit that the fruit of the Spirit can grow. As the hymn has it:

> Breathe on me, Breath of God;
> Fill me with life anew,
> That I may love what Thou dost love,
> And do what Thou wouldst do.

Or, as the children's hymn has it even more simply:

> Holy Spirit, help us
> Daily by Thy might,
> What is wrong to conquer,
> And to choose the right.

Peace comes through the Spirit (Romans 14[17]). It might well be said that peace is the deepest and the most universal desire of the human heart. Paul Tabori tells how in the days of the war he met in a café a much decorated French soldier who had newly gained another decoration. As they talked the soldier accidentally dropped a little St Anthony of Padua medallion. St Anthony's little medals are supposed to make the wishes of the wearer come true, just as St Christopher's medals are supposed to protect the traveller and the wayfarer. The wearer is supposed to wish his wish as he buys the little medal. Paul Tabori glanced at the medal. 'What was your wish?' he said to the soldier. The soldier answered: 'A strange wish for a soldier—peace.' That is the wish of every heart.

The amazing thing about the Holy Spirit is that, when a man becomes aware of the Spirit, and when a man seeks the Spirit in the only way in which the Spirit can be sought, peace comes—if the phrase be allowed—almost as a by-product. The Spirit can only be found in stillness and in waiting. The very practice of the presence of the Spirit brings into life the silence, the stillness, the relaxation of tension which life so tragically needs. Alan Walker, in *Everybody's Calvary*, tells of a man from the outback who came to the city of Sydney in Australia. His first question was: 'What is everyone running for?' There is an old Chinese parable which tells that someone once said to a flock of wild geese: 'If you will *all* be quiet I'll tell you something which will turn you into human beings.' And then one was quiet and another was quiet. But they were never *all* quiet at once; and the sage waited and waited, and grew grey and old as the days and the years went by, and in the end the geese were all caught and eaten.

The practice of the presence of the Holy Spirit brings the quietness which is like a healing dew on the spirit amidst the clamorous world; the practice of the presence of the Holy Spirit brings relaxation from that tension which is the biggest killer in modern life. And then something more happens—the practice of the presence of the Holy Spirit brings a new awareness of the constant presence of God, and into life there comes a new security, a new confidence that with God we can cope with life, a new power.

The peace of the Spirit is never negative; the peace of the Spirit is not a lethargic waiting. The peace of the Spirit is the peace of power. Sir William Watson paid a great tribute to Wordsworth in his poem, *Wordsworth's Grave:*

> *Not Milton's keen, translunar music thine;*
> *Not Shakespeare's cloudless, boundless human view;*
> *Not Shelley's flush of rose on peaks divine;*
> *Nor yet the wizard twilight Coleridge knew.*

> *What hadst thou that could make so large amends*
> *For all thou hadst not and thy peers possessed,*
> *Motion and fire, swift means to radiant ends?—*
> *Thou hadst, for weary feet, the gift of rest.*

From Shelley's dazzling glow or thunderous haze,
  From Byron's tempest-anger, tempest-mirth,
Men turned to thee and found—not blast and blaze,
  Tumult of tottering heavens, but peace on earth.

Nor peace that grows by Lethe, scentless flower,
  There in white languors to decline and cease;
But peace whose names are also rapture, power,
  Clear sight, and love: for these are parts of peace.

Peace and power—even the *seeking* of the Spirit brings that unique peace—how much more the *finding*?

Joy comes through the Spirit (Romans 14^{17}). The joy of the Spirit is the necessary complement and corollary of the peace of the Spirit. As we have seen, the peace of the Spirit is the peace of power. It is the peace of the man who has become aware that he is living in a presence which enables him to cope with anything. The really happy man is the man who has a task to do, and who knows that he can cope with that task, and that he can cope with any task which may be laid upon him. This is not self-conceit; it is confidence in God. The happy man is the man who knows that he can cope with any experience which life may bring to him. Such a man does not expect to avoid disappointment and sorrow and pain and loss, but he knows that within him he has the secret which will enable him to pass the breaking-point and not to break. Hugh Walpole's favourite maxim was: ' 'Tisn't life that matters, but the courage you bring to it', and the man of joy is the man who has found the secret of this courage. It was said of Cromwell's Ironsides: 'It was ever the fashion for Cromwell's pikemen to rejoice greatly when they beheld the enemy.' They rejoiced at the struggle with which they were confronted.

This is the joy which only the Spirit can give; for life in the Spirit is life in the constant awareness of, and experience of, the presence of God; and if God is with us, of whom then shall we be afraid?

Hope comes through the Spirit (Romans 15^{13}; Galatians 5^{5}).

God is the God of hope, and through the Spirit we may abound in hope. It is easy to be pessimistic about the future of the world and of mankind. 'Man', said H. G. Wells, 'who began in a cave behind a windbreak will end in the disease-soaked ruins of a slum.' Clemenceau, the great French states-man once said: 'Human beings are like apes who have stolen Jupiter's thunder. It is easy to see what will happen one of these days; they will kill one another to the last man. At most a dozen will escape, some Negroes in the Congo. Then they'll begin the story again, the same old story.' It is easy to be pessimistic about individual men or about ourselves, and to feel that improvement is impossible, that the habits which bind us are unconquerable, that the chains which fetter us are unbreakable, that we have no defence against the assaults of our temptations and the seduction of our sins.

That pessimism would be justified, it would indeed be inevitable, if man was solely responsible for the world or for himself and for his fellow-men. But if we believe in the Holy Spirit, then we believe that in the world there is another factor, there is 'a power not ourselves which makes for righteousness.' To believe in the Holy Spirit is to believe that there is abroad in the world the influence of God Himself, nay more, the presence and the action of God Himself. For that reason despair is forbidden. Men can hinder and delay, but men cannot entirely frustrate and defeat the eternal purposes of God.

Love comes through the Spirit (Romans 15[30]; Colossians 1[8]). W. B. Yeats spoke of the 'fall into division,' and the need of 'the resurrection into unity'. Love is the relationship which God intends and desires should exist between man and man. The love which Christ came to bring among men is the reflection of the universal benevolence of God, who sends His rain on the just and the unjust, and makes His sun to shine on the evil and the good. Christian love is not an emotional thing, with the ebb and flow which all emotional things must have. Christian love is that undefeatable goodwill which nothing can change to bitterness or hate. There exists a sheet of paper, written by Nurse Edith Cavell, and written immediately before she was shot for helping her fellow-countrymen to escape to Britain during the first World War. It runs like this:

Arrested—[the date]; Tried—[the date]; condemned—[the date]. Shot at seven in the morning of 12th October 1915. With love. E.C.

With love, Edith Cavell could say under even those circumstances; the Christian life must be *with love*.

If that is ever to happen, there must come into the hearts of men what we call a new spirit; and that spirit is the Holy Spirit. The Holy Spirit not only unites men to God; He unites men to one another. Life in the Spirit is life in the conscious awareness of God; and he who is consciously aware of God can never hate. We only hate when we have forgotten God.

Liberty comes through the Spirit (2 Corinthians 3[17]). Where the Spirit of the Lord is, there is liberty. At least two kinds of liberty are the work of the Spirit. First there is liberty from legalism and law. Where the Spirit is, men no longer deal with any situation or with any person in a hard, rigid, unsympathetic, unimaginative, hidebound legalism; they are not bound by rules and precedents and regulations; they deal with all things in the Spirit of Jesus Christ. Second, there is liberty from the disunity within oneself. It is only when the Spirit enters into a man's heart, and takes possession of him, and rules and dominates him that the warring disunity of human nature becomes a harmony. It is only then that a man ceases to be a walking civil war, and has liberty and freedom to become a person.

Strength comes through the Spirit (Ephesians 3[16]). It is through the Spirit that we are strengthened in the inner man. The constant tragedy of life is not that we do not know what we ought to do, not that we are unaware of the possibilities within us, but that we are consistently unable to put that knowledge into action, and to transfer those possibilities into realities. Edwin Muir in his autobiography has a quotation from his own diaries: 'After a certain age all of us, good and bad, are guilt-stricken because of powers within us which have never been realized; because, in other words, we are not what we should be.' He goes on: 'I am astonished at the contrast between the power I am aware of in me and the triteness of my life. As I grow older I feel more and more the need to make that barren astonishment effectual, to wrest some palpable prize from it; for I cannot see that the astonishment itself is any use to me.' That is an experience of which we all know something.

At the Missionary Conference in Edinburgh in 1910, John R. Mott said: 'It is a dangerous thing to glow with a knowledge of the needs of men, to be swept by generous emotions, if that knowledge and that emotion do not issue in genuine action. Let the end of the conference be the beginning of conquest.' Nobly said—but how? Upton Sinclair, novelist and reformer, once said: 'First I portray events; then I try to make them happen.' The difficulty lies never in portraying them, but always in seeking to make them happen. John Drinkwater wrote:

> *Grant us the will to fashion as we feel,*
> *Grant us the strength to labour as we know,*
> *Grant us the purpose, ribbed and edged with steel,*
>   *To strike the blow.*
>
> *Knowledge we ask not; knowledge Thou hast lent;*
> *But Lord, the will, there lies our deepest need;*
> *Grant us the strength to build above the deep intent*
>   *The deed, the deed.*

Here is the very function of the Spirit. More than once the idea of the Spirit in Paul's letters is identified with the idea of power (Romans $15^{13, 19}$; 1 Corinthians 2^4; 1 Thessalonians 1^5). The Spirit is the dynamic. Men of the Spirit not only dream their dreams and see their visions; they are also men of action, men who do things and get things done.

The only person who can give us this strength is the Spirit.

That is why no man can be a man of action unless he is first a man of prayer. Whatever resolutions we make, whatever plans we form, they will be futile, unless after the resolving and after the planning there comes the waiting for the Spirit.

Such, then, are the great things which in the experience of Paul come through the Spirit. Ebenezer Erskine once said of the great experience in which he found Jesus Christ: 'That night I got my head out of time into eternity.' When we experience the Spirit, even in this world of space and time we experience eternity and God.

There are certain words and expressions which Paul uses of the Christian's relationship to the Spirit, all of which have vivid and significant pictures in them.

The Christian *lives* in the Spirit (Galatians 5²⁵). For the Christian the Spirit is the very air which he breathes and without which he cannot go on living. It must always be remembered that this kind of picture is even more vivid in Greek than it is in English. The Greek word for Spirit, *pneuma*, is in fact the Greek word for *breath*; and, therefore, in Greek the picture is that for the Christian the Spirit is the very breath of life. The experience of the Spirit changes existence into life.

The Spirit *dwells in* the Christian (Romans 8⁹, ¹¹; 1 Corinthians 3¹⁶⁻¹⁷). The Christian is *filled with* the Spirit (Ephesians 5¹⁸). The Christian is the *temple* of the Holy Spirit (1 Corinthians 6¹⁹). This means nothing less than that the Christian is himself the Holy of Holies in which the Spirit of God dwells. If the connection between man and the Spirit of God is as close as this, then certain things follow. As William Blake has it: 'All that lives is holy.' The breath of God and the Spirit of God—in Greek the words would be exactly the same —are in every man.

That great truth must change our attitude to ourselves. W. B. Yeats tells how a friend of his, Macgregor Matthew, had what he calls 'a medicinal phrase to repeat in moments of adversity'—'There is no part of me that is not of the gods'. Surely, when a man realizes that, he cannot defile the divinity that is within him. Surely he must have a new idea of what life means. If his body is the temple of the Holy Spirit, he cannot defile it, and abuse it, and injure it with low and polluted things. If his mind is the dwelling-place of the Holy Spirit, surely his thoughts must be clean. If his heart is the place where the Holy Spirit enters and remains, surely he must cleanse himself of all unclean desires. To be the dwelling-place of the Holy Spirit is not only the privilege of manhood, it is also the responsibility of manhood. When a guest comes to stay with us, we give him the best that our house can supply. What if that guest be God? And what if the place where God in His Spirit takes up his dwelling-place be nothing less than our own bodies, and our own selves?

But, further, the fact that manhood is the dwelling-place of the Spirit of God must affect our relationship to our own fellow-men. Contempt, arrogance, intolerance are no longer possible for those in whom the Spirit of God dwells. Douglas Downes was famous as the apostle to the tramps and the outcasts of England. He was able and willing to enter into a relationship of friendship and fellowship with any man. Once in a Welsh mining valley he was challenged by a group of young and embittered miners to discuss the Christian faith. They did not even expect him to accept the invitation, but he did. The talk was of God. One of the young men challenged him. 'Tell us', said the miner, 'can you see God?' 'Yes', said Downes, 'I can see Him now. I can see Him in your eyes.' The Christian is the man who always sees God in other men; that is precisely what compels him to be a missionary; that is why contempt is the most unchristian and unchristlike of all sins.

If men are the temple of the Holy Spirit, then we must reverence both ourselves and our fellow-men. It becomes a bounden duty to live in purity and in charity, to respect ourselves and to respect others.

The Christian is *led by* the Spirit, and the Christian *walks in* the Spirit (Galatians 5[16, 18, 25]). If the Christian is led by the Spirit, it means that all his decisions are taken in the guidance of the Spirit. But it is well to remember that a friend cannot give us his advice and his guidance until we seek it, and the guidance of the Spirit is something to which we must open ourselves, and for which we must ask and wait.

In Galatians 5[16] and 5[25] the Authorized Version uses the same word to translate two different Greek words. '*Walk* in the Spirit.' 'Let us also *walk* in the Spirit.' In the first instance the Greek word is *peripatein*, which literally means *to walk around*, *to walk about*, and which became the regular word for a man's life and conduct in everyday life. This means that every action in every day life, at home, in business, in study, in work, in pleasure, must be lived in the awareness of the presence of the Spirit. In the second instance the word is *stoichein; stoichos* means a *line* or a *file* of soldiers, and the word commonly means *to march in file*, to march in step as soldiers march. This word describes what we might call concerted action, action in joint effort. It is as if Paul said: 'When you set out upon any concerted action with your fellow-men, let the Holy Spirit be the person at whose word of command you march in step with one another.' It is the same picture as the hymn has:

> *Like a mighty army*
> *Moves the Church of God.*

When we put both these passages in Galatians together, we have a double picture. The Holy Spirit is the guide and the director of our personal life, our personal decisions, and our personal actions; and the Holy Spirit is the person who disciplines and orders us, when we engage in concerted action in the company of our fellow-men. That is to say, the Holy Spirit is He who enables us to live in personal honour and purity, and the Holy Spirit is He who enables us to live in unity and in harmony with our fellow-men. When we make mistakes in the ordering of our own life, and when our personal relationships with others break down, it means that we have not asked, and waited for, and accepted the guidance of the Spirit of God.

The Christian *stands fast* in the Holy Spirit (Philippians

1²⁷). It is in the power of the Spirit that he is enabled to maintain his loyalty and his witness to Jesus Christ, when loyalty and witness are both difficult and dangerous. Robert Louis Stevenson speaks of the necessity of bearing 'nae shauchlin' testimony', no wavering testimony. The Spirit will give a man wisdom to defend and to present his faith in argument, power to witness to it by life and action, and courage to hold to it when it is under fire.

The Christian can *grieve* the Holy Spirit (Ephesians 4³⁰). If the Christian lives in impurity, or in bitterness and unforgivingness with his fellow-men, he thereby grieves the Holy Spirit. To sin is not only to break God's law, it is also to break God's heart.

The Christian can *quench* the Holy Spirit (1 Thessalonians 5¹⁹). Deafness to the voice of the Spirit, unreceptiveness to the message of the Spirit, suspicion or disregard of the methods and ways of the Spirit, can, as it were, extinguish the flame of the Spirit. The Christian can make himself such that he cannot receive the gifts the Spirit brings.

So far we have been studying the work of the Spirit in the life of the individual Christian, but Paul has also much to say about the work of the Spirit in the life of the Church as a whole.

The Spirit is, what we might well call *the guardian of the creed of the Church*. The Spirit will never move a man to say that Jesus is accursed, and only through the Spirit is a man enabled to say that Jesus is Lord (1 Corinthians 12³). The creed of the Church is the revelation of the Spirit. That is to say, there is an ultimate basis of Christian belief which is not the intellectual discovery of the mind of man, but which is the revelation of God, brought to man through the Spirit of God. There is a passage in the Revelation on which H. B. Swete has an interesting comment to make. In the picture of the victorious appearance of the warrior Christ, the John of the Revelation says that His eyes are like a flame of fire, and that He has many royal crowns on His head. Then John goes on to say that 'He has a name written which no one knows except

Himself (Revelation 19^{12}). Throughout the ages there has been much speculation about that unknown name. But Swete sees a certain symbolism in this picture: 'Notwithstanding the dogmatic helps which the Church offers, the mind fails to grasp the inmost significance of the Person of Christ, which eludes all efforts to bring it within the terms of human knowledge. Only the Son of God can understand the mystery of His own being.' There is in Jesus Christ an ultimate mystery, which the mind cannot comprehend, and before which we can only worship and adore. When we say, 'Jesus Christ is Lord', we are giving utterance, not to that which the human mind discovered, but to that which the Spirit revealed. There is much that a man can find, but there is an ultimate mystery which he can only receive. This is far from saying that the Christian must not think for himself, and think deeply, and think strenuously; but it is to say that, before we think, we should do well to listen, for in the last analysis our thought is not about that which we have discovered, but about that which the Spirit has revealed. The strenuous activity of thought begins from the stillness of meditation, contemplation and prayer.

From the Spirit there comes *the diversity of gifts within the Church* (1 Corinthians 12$^{8-11}$). The word of wisdom, the word of knowledge, faith, the gift of healing, the power to work miracles, the ability to prophesy, the power of discernment, the gift of tongues, the gift of interpretation—all these, says Paul, are the gifts of the Spirit. The Spirit distributes His gifts to each man, as He will.

There is something here which we should do well to remember. There is a tendency to think of spiritual gifts in terms of what we might call the work of the professional ministry, to think of them in terms of preaching, praying, teaching, pastoral visitation. It is the teaching of Paul that every gift which is needed for the successful operation of the Church is a gift of the Spirit. The gift of the craftsman who works with his hands, of the secretary who works with pen or typewriter, of the organizer and the administrator, of those

who care for the cleanliness of the buildings of the Church—
all these are gifts of the Spirit. As Mrs Browning put it: 'All
service ranks the same with God. One of the greatest losses
which the passing of the centuries has brought to the Church
is the loss of the craftsman. The craftsman would be rediscovered in the Church, his gifts would be rededicated to
the Church, if we would stop erecting a false spiritual aris-
tocracy, if we would remember that word *ministry* simply
means *service*, and if we would remember that any gift which
a man has is a gift of the Spirit, and can be laid on the altar of
the service of God.

From the Spirit there comes *the unity of the Church*. There
is a kaleidoscopic diversity in spiritual gifts, but all these gifts
are welded into an harmonious unity by the work of the Spirit
(1 Corinthians 12⁴). There are many gifts, but there is the
same Spirit. It is the Spirit who brings it about that this
diversity of gifts does not lead to competition, but to harmony.
The Spirit is the creator of fellowship within the Church. In
the words of the blessing, we speak of 'the fellowship of the
Holy Spirit' (2 Corinthians 13¹⁴). The word for fellowship is
koinōnia. Originally that was a word of business and secular
Greek, and meant *partnership*. 'The fellowship of the Spirit'
means the fellowship, the partnership, which the Spirit alone
can give.

It is to that fellowship which only the Spirit can make
possible that Paul appeals when he is urging the Philippians to
show the same obedience and humility as Jesus Christ demonstrated in His life (Philippians 2¹). It is in that fellowship of
the Spirit that the Philippians are to stand fast (Philippians
1²⁷). They are not standing as isolated units, but as members
of a fellowship in the Spirit. It is the Spirit who brings that
unity in which Jew and Greek together worship Christ, and
in which the barriers are broken down (Ephesians 2¹⁸). It is
in and by the Spirit that the people of Christ are builded
together for a habitation for God (Ephesians 2²²). The unity
of the Spirit comes from the fact that there is one body and
one Spirit (Ephesians 4³, ⁴).

We live in days when there is much talk of ecumenicity, and when there is a longing and a desire to reunite the divisions in the Church which is the Body of Christ. We shall not get far along that road, unless we remember that the consistent teaching of the New Testament is that the Spirit—if the phrase will be allowed—is the divine cement which holds all the structure of the Church together. The unity of the Church is not a unity of organization, administration, government; the unity of the Church comes from the fact that the one Spirit pervades the whole Church. The forgetting of systems and the rediscovery of the Spirit is the only way to true Christian fellowship. A warring congregation and a divided Church are a congregation and a Church in which the Spirit has been denied His place. There can be few things which grieve the Spirit so bitterly as a congregation, which ought to be a fellowship, torn by disputes which arise because men listen to the thoughts and desires of their own minds and hearts rather than to the pleadings of the Spirit.

It is the Spirit who *guides decisions within the Church.* When Paul has given his decisions on the complicated problems which have been troubling the Church at Corinth, his only claim is: 'I think also that I have the Spirit of God' (1 Corinthians 7[40]). He does not claim to decide as an expert in Church law; his only claim is that he is a man of the Spirit. And it is a fact of Christian experience that men remember a saint long after an ecclesiastic is forgotten.

The true *worship* of God is in the Spirit (Philippians 3[3]). Worship is not primarily a matter of edifices or liturgies; it is primarily a matter of the Spirit. Where the Spirit is absent, all forms of worship are futile and unavailing; where the Spirit is present, men know that they are in the presence of God.

It may be that the loveliest and most precious of all Paul's thoughts about the Spirit is his thought about the place of the Spirit in our prayers. Paul speaks of that place in Romans 8[26, 27], which we give in the Moffatt translation: 'So too the Spirit assists us in our weakness; for we do not know how to pray aright, but the Spirit pleads for us with sighs that are beyond words, and He who searches the human heart knows what is in the mind of the Spirit, since the Spirit pleads before God for the saints.' The idea behind that passage, as Dr C. H. Dodd magnificently expounds it, is this.

By ourselves we cannot pray aright, because we do not know what to ask for. We do not know what to ask for because we cannot see a day, or even an hour, ahead, and because, even in any given situation, we do not know what is best for us. Even the Greeks knew that. Socrates used to teach his disciples to pray only for good things, but never to specify what those good things were, but to leave that to God. If that be so, how can we pray at all? Pray we must, for prayer is 'the divine in us appealing to the God above us.' As Paul sees it, all we can do is to bring to God an inarticulate sigh of appeal, and the Holy Spirit will translate that sigh of ours to God. Here is the noblest of all conceptions of the Spirit. We *must* pray; we do not know for what to pray; all we can do is to take to God the desperate, voiceless longing of the human heart, the inarticulate, wordless sigh; and when that happens, the Spirit is there to take our prayer and to place it before God as it ought to be prayed. The Spirit is the interpreter of the prayers of men. It is the wonder of the Spirit that the Spirit not only brings God to men, but also brings men to God. So often in prayer all words seem inadequate; so often, when life is at its most bewildering and its most wounding and heart-breaking, there is nothing but a dumb longing for God. That is prayer at its highest; and that is when the Spirit breaks in and interprets and translates our prayer to God.

Finally, we may note two things to which in the letters of Paul the Spirit is always opposed and contrasted. ·

The Spirit is contrasted with *the flesh* (Romans 8[1,4, 9, 13]; Galatians 3[2], 5[17], 6[8]). Spirit and flesh are at war with each other; the task of the Christian is to walk, not after the flesh, but after the Spirit. Here we come upon the eternal division between two elements in human nature. In every man there is the ape and the angel, the devilish and the divine, the saint and the sinner. Long ago the Jewish teachers taught the doctrine of the two natures, the *yetzer hatob*, the good nature, and the *yetzer hara*, the evil nature. In man, they said, there are two opposing and contrasting and conflicting natures. Or they said that every man has two angels, a good angel on his right hand always inviting him to higher things, and an evil angel on his left hand always seeking to seduce him to lower things. One of the most famous pictures in the world is that drawn by Plato, when he describes the soul as a charioteer whose task it is to drive two horses in double harness. The one horse is tame, gentle, and obedient, and its name is reason; the other horse is wild, uncontrolled and undisciplined, and its name is passion. There again there is the picture of the conflict in human nature. Robert Burns wrote of his own life: 'My life reminded me of a ruined temple. What strength, what proportion in some parts! What unsightly gaps, what prostrate ruins in others!'

When Paul spoke of the *flesh*, he did not mean the body. When he spoke of the works and sins of the flesh, he did not mean what we commonly call fleshly sins, that is sexual sins and sins of the bodily passions. With the sins of the flesh Paul included such things as hatred, wrath, strife, envy, heresy (Galatians 5[19-21]). By the flesh Paul meant that part of human nature which gives a bridgehead to sin. He meant these tendencies in man whose influence is downwards and away from God. He meant what the Jew would have called the evil nature.

It is precisely to that that the Spirit is opposed. The flesh is that within us which presents sin with an opportunity to defeat us and to lower us and to take us farther and farther from God. The Spirit is He who lifts us higher and higher and who brings us nearer God.

Here life presents us with an eternal choice. To which shall we listen? Shall we listen to the demands and the desires of what Paul calls the flesh? Or shall we listen to the invitations and encouragements of the Spirit? The great responsibility of human nature is that we can allow ourselves to be dominated by the flesh or by the Spirit. And the great possibility of human nature is that, if we accept the government of the Spirit, then even the flesh can be cleansed and purified and brought into the service of God.

The second great opposition and contrast in the thought of Paul is between the Spirit and *the letter of the law* (Romans 2²⁹; 1 Corinthians 3⁶; Galatians 3²). It is the letter that kills, and the Spirit who gives life. In every sphere of life there is the contrast between the man who judges everything by the letter of the law, the legalist, and the man who judges by the Spirit.

Once in Edinburgh in the hearing of Burns, a clergyman adversely criticized Gray's *Elegy*, a poem of which Burns was very fond. Burns defended it. But the clergyman continued his attacks upon it, although he could not even quote it correctly. Burns bore the quibblings and the nigglings as long as he could; then he said: 'Sir, I now perceive that a man may be an excellent judge of poetry by square and rule, and be after all a damned blockhead.' Here is the difference between judging by the letter and by the Spirit.

The difference between judging by the letter and the Spirit lies simply in this. Are we to find our standards of judgement in some book of rules and regulations and laws? Or, are we to find our standards of judgement in a living person? The great example of this is Jesus Himself. When the woman who was taken in adultery was brought before Him (John 8¹⁻¹¹), those who wished to stone her to death were, according to the letter of the law, perfectly right. The law is stated clearly enough in Leviticus 20¹⁰ and in Deuteronomy 22²². The letter of the law was quite clear—the woman ought to die. But Jesus did not judge that woman by the letter of the law; He judged her by the love of God.

Again and again, life will confront us with the choice of observing the letter of the law or following the guidance of the Spirit. That is not by any means to say that these two things will always be different. It is not even enough in any human situation to say: 'The Bible says . . .' The only thing that is enough is to say: 'Lord Jesus, what wilt Thou have me to do?'

It is true that in God's book the Christian has the letter of the law; but the fact remains that the Christian has more—he has the living presence of Jesus Christ. And the Christian settles his problems and makes his decisions, not by reference to any book, but by reference to a living person, by reference to his Lord.

When we study the letters of Paul, we come to see that the basic fact of the Christian life is that there can be no such thing as a Christian life without the Spirit. Without the Spirit a man can be right neither with himself, nor with his fellow-men, nor with God.

CHAPTER SIX

The Holy Spirit in the Life and Thought of the New Testament Church

WE HAVE studied the teaching about the Holy Spirit in the Synoptic Gospels, in the Fourth Gospel, in Acts, and in the Letters of Paul. Our plan in this chapter is to examine the material about the Holy Spirit in the rest of the New Testament, so that from it we may construct a picture of the place of the Spirit in the thought and in the life of the New Testament Church.

The Holy Spirit is specially connected with the Scriptures, that is, with the Old Testament, which at that time was the only Bible which the Church possessed. Again and again, when a quotation from the Old Testament is cited, it is cited as a word spoken by the Holy Spirit. So quotations are introduced by the words, 'The Holy Spirit says' (1 Timothy 4[1]; Hebrews 3[7]). 'The Holy Spirit indicates' (Hebrews 9[8]), 'The Holy Spirit witnesses' (Hebrews 10[15]). Similarly, it was the Spirit of Christ who inspired the prophets who foretold the sufferings of Christ (1 Peter 1[11]). Indeed no prophecy is of merely human impulse, for in the Scriptures men moved by the Holy Spirit spoke from God (2 Peter 1[21]). The New Testament Church regarded the words of Scripture as the direct message of God.

This is not the time or the place to enter into a discussion of what is meant by the inspiration of Scripture. But there is one question which we may well ask. In what sense did the New Testament Church regard the words of Scripture as being inspired as contrasted with the words of any other great book, any other great production of the human spirit, any other writing which has illuminated the minds and moved the hearts of men? Burns, for instance, says of himself: 'The poetic genius of my country found me, as the prophetic bard did Elisha, at the plough, and threw her inspiring mantle over me. She bade me sing the loves, the joys, the rural scenes and rural pleasures of my native tongue. I tuned my wild, artless notes as she inspired.' Wherein lies the basic difference between the inspiration of the poet, an inspiration of which he was deeply conscious, and the inspiration which the New Testament Church found in Scripture? It may well be that we must find the difference in the *purpose* of the inspiration. The inspiration of other writers may be designed to bring delight to the ears and hearts of men, to bring them knowledge, to ease the burden of the world; the inspiration of Scripture is unique in being designed to tell the story and the offer and the conditions of God's salvation for men. In the Bible alone the New Testament Church found the record of the salvation of God which culminated in Jesus Christ. The Bible to the New Testament Church, as it must still be to the Church in any age, is the Book of books, because in it alone there is the story of salvation and the record of the Saviour. The uniqueness of the Bible lies in the fact that it is the record of the saving events of God, long planned, long foretold, and ending in Jesus Christ.

It was the experience of the New Testament Church that the power which renews men is the power of the Spirit. We are saved not by works of righteousness, but, in the mercy of God, by the washing of regeneration and by the renewing power of the Spirit, which God sheds abundantly on us through Jesus Christ our Lord (Titus 3⁵). The Spirit of God, who was God's agent in creation, is also God's agent in recreation (Genesis 1²).

Here is that for which the pagan world was crying out. The pagan world was hauntingly conscious of goodness and desperately conscious of sin; and at the same time it was despairingly aware that there was no possible way from sin to goodness. It had a dream which it could not in any way realize; it was conscious of a disease for which it could see no possible cure. Men, said Seneca, hate their sins and love them at the same time; the consequence was that, however much they loathed them, they could not leave them. Epictetus spoke of men's 'weakness in necessary things'. Quintilian called Seneca 'a splendid assailant of the faults of men'; Seneca said of himself: 'This is the one goal of my days and of my nights—to put an end to my old faults'; and yet in spite of it all, Seneca could call himself *homo non tolerabilis*, a man not to be tolerated. He writes: 'We have all sinned, some more, some less, some deliberately, some by accident, some by the fault of others; we have not stood bravely enough by our good resolutions. Nor is it only that we have done wrong; we shall be so to the end.' Persius speaks of 'filthy Natta numbed with vice', and says of the guilty: 'Let them see virtue, and pine that they have lost her for ever.' Epictetus, in T. R. Glover's phrase, talks of 'the necrosis of the soul'. The ancient world well knew its condition, but there was nothing and no one to whom it could look for renewal.

Here is exactly what the Holy Spirit offered, and still offers. One of the labours of Hercules was to cleanse the stables of Augeas. In them Augeas had stabled 3,000 head of oxen for thirty years, without ever once cleaning them out. It was the task of Hercules to clear away this vast accumulation of filth. He did not even attempt to do it himself. He deflected the course of two rivers so that they flowed through the stables, and their cleansing tide did what no human effort could have done. The Holy Spirit links a man with a power far greater than his own, and that flood tide of cleansing and of renewing does for him what he himself could never do. The most triumphant statement in Paul's letters is made concerning the most notoriously immoral of ancient cities. In writing to Corinth Paul makes a list of sinners—fornicators, idolaters, adulterers, effeminate, homosexuals, thieves, covetous, drunkards, revilers, extortioners—and then come the words, 'And such were some of you' (1 Corinthians 6[9-11]). That is the work of the Holy Spirit. The Holy Spirit, as the New

Testament Church saw it, is the cleansing, recreating, purifying, flood of the power and the presence of God, whereby
a man, however evil, however bound by the chains and fetters
of sin, is made a good man. Denney once remarked that, to
put it at its simplest, the task of Christianity is to make bad
men good—and that is what the Holy Spirit does.

We may put this in another way—the Holy Spirit is the
agent of sanctification. The Christian is sanctified by the
Spirit for obedience to Jesus Christ (1 Peter 1²). The word
for sanctification is *hagiasmos*. All Greek names ending in *-asmos*
describe a process, and not a finished event. *Hagiasmos*,
therefore, may best be translated *the road to holiness*. *Hagiasmos* is the noun which is connected with *hagios*, the word
which is generally translated *holy*, and which is also the word
for the people whom the New Testament calls *saints*. In the
New Testament the basic idea of the word holy is 'different'.
The Sabbath day is holy because it is different from other
days; the Temple is holy because it is different from other
buildings; a sacrificial victim is holy because it is different
from other animals; God is supremely holy because He is
different from men. A *saint* in the New Testament sense
is, therefore, a man in whom there is this quality of difference.
That difference is something which is unattainable in our own
power. The Holy Spirit is the person through whose power
upon us we can day by day walk the road to holiness, day by
day acquiring more of this quality of difference, day by day
becoming more and more *hagios*, that is, more and more like
God. But, we must note, this change is not an effortless thing
on our part. We are sanctified *for obedience*. It is a power
which demands our own effort, our own self-discipline, as the
price of its co-operation. When our will begins to co-operate
with the power of the Holy Spirit, then things happen in life.

It follows from this that the possession of the Holy Spirit,
the demonstration in life and living of the power of the Spirit,
is the very proof and guarantee of the Christian life. One of
the great, indisputable guarantees of the reality of salvation
is God's gifts of the Holy Spirit distributed among His people

(Hebrews 2⁴). To become a mature Christian is nothing other than to become more and more deeply a sharer and partaker in the Holy Spirit (Hebrews 6⁴).

Here is something which the ancient world, to which Christianity first came, could fully understand. In that world moral standards and imperial empires were alike collapsing; it was a world where the foundations were being shaken. As T. R. Glover put it, what was needed was the linking of the individual to something which could not be shaken. It was precisely this that the basic belief of Stoicism had tried to effect. The Stoics believed that God was fiery spirit of a clearness and fineness and purity that could never be found upon earth; and they believed that that which gave every man life was that a particle, a spark, a *scintilla*, of that divine fire; which was God, dwelt within his body. It was thus that the Stoics sought to find the link between man and God. H. G. Wells in one of his novels tells of a man for whom life was too much, and who was in imminent danger of physical and mental collapse. He felt that his only hope of rescue was to get hold of something bigger than himself and identify himself with that. That is the instinctive desire of the human heart; and that is exactly what is offered to us in the Holy Spirit. The Holy Spirit is He who enables us to identify ourselves with God through Jesus Christ.

If the guarantee of Christianity is the possession of the Spirit, then equally clearly a man cannot be a Christian without the Spirit. In Jude's short letter there is a test. Those who are worldly, those who are scoffers, and those who are the causes of division have not the Spirit (Jude 19). The materialist and the cynic have no experience of the Spirit. And we should do well to remember that the man who in any fellowship and in any congregation has been the cause of difference and division has thereby demonstrated that he does not possess, and is not possessed by, the Spirit.

In the material which we are studying, the Spirit is called by two names. The Spirit is called the Spirit of grace (Hebrews 10²⁹) and the Spirit is said to be truth (1 John 5⁶). It is part of the wonder of the Spirit that in Him there is combined grace and truth. There is a certain graciousness and a certain kindliness which shuts its eyes to the truth; it refuses to see the faults and the sins and the mistakes of others, but rather draws a comfortable veil across them. There is on the other hand the kind of person who is devoted to truth, and who, therefore, pitilessly, unsparingly and even scarifyingly unveils, reveals and condemns the errors and the mistakes and the faults of others. The wonder of God and of His Spirit is that in Him grace and truth are uniquely combined, so that in His truth God sees the sin of man, and in His grace finds its cure.

It was the conviction of the New Testament Church that persecution and trial nobly and gallantly borne brought upon a man a still greater measure of the Spirit (1 Peter 4[14]). When a man suffers reproach for the name of Jesus Christ, he is blessed, for then the Spirit of glory and of God rests upon him. 'God', said Seneca, 'has the mind of a father towards good men, and loves them strenuously. "Let them," He says, "be exercised in work, pain and loss, that they may gather true strength." ' As T. R. Glover puts it, translating the thought of Seneca: 'It is because God is in love with the good that he gives them fortune to wrestle with. There is a match worth God's sight—a brave man paired with evil fortune especially if the good man himself is the challenger.' It was the strong belief of the Christians of the New Testament Church—and in truth they had to suffer and to resist even unto death—that suffering and sorrow and reproach for Christ do not separate a man from God, but bring to him an even greater experience of the Spirit, if he meets them courageously.

The New Testament Church was convinced that the Holy Spirit has everything to do both with the discovery and the transmission of the orthodox faith and belief of the Church. Only through the Spirit can a man confess that Jesus Christ is come in the flesh; and anyone who denies that is under the influence of a spirit who is not the Spirit of God (1 John 4[2]). The revelation of the true faith is the work of the Spirit.

But even more interesting is what the New Testament has

to say about the transmission of the faith. It is our duty to keep, by the Holy Spirit who dwells in us, the good thing which has been committed to us (2 Timothy 1¹⁴). There is something of the first importance here. In Greek *the good thing which has been committed to us* is the *parathēkē*. *Parathēkē* is a Greek business word meaning a *deposit*. The picture is that a man who, going on a journey or contemplating an absence, deposits his possessions with a trusted friend. And to the Greek there was no more sacred duty in this world than the return of that deposit safe and intact. There is a Greek story, found in many classical authors, which stresses this responsibility. A certain Spartan called Glaucus had a reputation for justice. To him came a man from Miletus, who had turned half his fortune into silver, and who, knowing the reputation of Glaucus for absolute honesty, wished to deposit it with him. This he did, and he gave Glaucus tokens by which the right claimant to the deposit might be recognized when the time to claim it came. The years passed on, and in due time the two sons of the man of Miletus came to claim the fortune, bringing the tokens to establish their identity. Glaucus declared that he had no recollection of ever having been entrusted with the deposit, and asked for four months to seek to bring it back to his memory, if indeed the transaction had ever happened at all. Glaucus well knew that he had received the silver, and well knew that he ought to restore it. He consulted the oracle at Delphi to see what he ought to do, and the oracle gave him a dreadful warning of what happened to the man who had been entrusted with a deposit and failed to return it. In terror Glaucus sent for the two sons of the man of Miletus and restored the silver to them. But even then disaster fell upon him because he had even contemplated the possibility of being false. 'There is at this day no descendant of Glaucus, nor any household that bears Glaucus' name; he and his have been uprooted out of Sparta. So good a thing it is not even to design aught concerning a trust, save the restoring of it on demand' (Herodotus, 6. 86). To a Greek the restoration of a trust was an obligation of the utmost sanctity,

and in Jewish law also there was a similar binding obligation
(Exodus 22$^{2-13}$; Leviticus 6$^{3-7}$).

Here in the Pastoral Epistles the faith is called the *parathēkē*;
it is the sacred trust which has to be handed on from generation to generation. It must never be lost or abandoned; it
must never be adulterated or distorted; it must be handed on
in all its purity and in all its splendour.

He who enables us to hand on the faith is the Holy Spirit.
Now the Holy Spirit is a living, acting, energizing, illuminating person, and the faith, therefore, is not something static,
committed to print in a book, or crystallized for ever in some
credal declaration. If the faith is in the care of the Holy
Spirit, then the faith can never be a static thing. It is dynamic,
developing, flowering. What is wanted is not the handing on
of a dead and lifeless orthodoxy, petrified in some form of
words, antiquated in some set of categories. If the Holy
Spirit is the agent through whom the faith is handed on, then
it may well be that to hand on the faith unaltered, unchanged,
undeveloped, unadapted to new worlds and categories of
thought is the sin against the Holy Spirit. A faith directed and
protected by the Holy Spirit is necessarily a faith re-thought,
re-expressed, re-minted in each generation. The man who
hands on the faith must not be like the servant who buried the
talent in the ground and handed it back unaltered and unused;
he must rather be like the men who made the five talents ten,
and the two talents four. He must add to the riches which he
has received.

It is through the Holy Spirit that a man first enters into the
faith; it is through the Holy Spirit that the faith is a dynamic-
ally developing force; it is through the Holy Spirit that the
faith is handed on from generation to generation.

The New Testament Church was sure that true preaching
was preaching through the Holy Spirit. Peter reminds his
people of those who preached the good news to them through
the Holy Spirit sent from heaven (1 Peter 1^{12}). Preaching is
not the expression of a man's opinions; it is not the airing of
a man's doubts; it is not the parade of a man's intellectual

knowledge and learning. Preaching is the message which the Holy Spirit has given to a man to deliver to the people of God.

It was said of one great preacher that when he was preaching ever and again he paused 'as if listening for a voice.' Jupiter Carlyle said of John Brown of Haddington: 'That man spoke as if he was conscious that the Son of God stood at his elbow.'

We must be quite clear what this means. If we say that a man's message is given to him by the Holy Spirit, that does not for one moment mean that a man is freed from study, freed from preparation, freed from discipline, freed from the most strenuous exercise of the mind which God has given him. The truth is that the more a man uses his own mind, the more the Holy Spirit will speak to him. The more a man studies Scripture with every help which scholarship can give him, the more the Holy Spirit will shine upon the pages of Scripture, and illuminate them, so that there will emerge from them flashes of truth which he has hitherto never seen. Jesus said: Unto every one that hath shall be given, and he shall have abundance; but from him that hath not shall be taken away even that which he hath (Matthew 25[29]). This may seem a hard saying, but it is a law of life. The more a man knows, the more he is capable of knowing. If a man grows lazy in mind or body, he loses even the ability of the craft that he once had. The harder a man works and thinks and studies to find out the meaning of the word of God, the more the Holy Spirit can reveal to him. The more a man allows his mind to grow slack and lazy and flabby, the less the Holy Spirit can say to him. True preaching comes when the loving heart and the disciplined mind are laid at the disposal of the Holy Spirit.

Prayer is in the Holy Spirit. A man must build himself up in the most holy faith by praying in the Holy Spirit (Jude 20). One of the strangest things about prayer is that it can be the most selfish activity in the world. Prayer can be merely seeking to use God for one's own purposes. We do not pray properly until we have first opened ourselves to the Holy

Spirit, for only under His guidance can we know what to pray for. When we learn to pray in the Spirit, we shall truly pray, 'Thy will be done,' not, 'Thy will be changed.' We shall truly ask God what He wishes us to do, and not tell God what we wish Him to do.

It is in the Revelation that we find one of the completest presentations of the work of the Holy Spirit. In that book we find that the Spirit has four great functions.

The Spirit is *the giver of the vision*. It is always when he is in the Spirit that the great visions flash upon the eyes of John (Revelation 1^{10}, 4^2, 17^3, 21^{10}). It is through the Spirit that even on earth a man is given a sight of heaven.

The Spirit is *the bringer of the message*. In each of the letters to the seven Churches, the hearers and readers are urged to hear what the Spirit is saying to the Churches (Revelation 2$^{7, 11, 17, 29}$, 3$^{6, 13, 22}$). The words of these letters are the words of the Risen Christ, but the bearer of the words is the Spirit. The Spirit is Christ's messenger to men.

The Spirit is *the guarantor of the promise*. In Revelation 14^{13}, we read the promise and the guarantee: 'Blessed are the dead who die in the Lord henceforth.' 'Blessed, indeed, says the Spirit, that they may rest from their labours, for their deeds follow them.' First, there comes the statement, and then there comes the guarantee of the Spirit. It is the Spirit within our hearts who assures us that the promises of God are true.

The Spirit is *the bearer of the invitation*. The Spirit and the Bride say, Come (Revelation 22^{17}). The Bride is the Church, and the Spirit and the Church unite in bearing to men the invitation of Jesus Christ. The vision, the message, the promise, the invitation, are all conveyed to men by the Spirit.

We have not in this book greatly, if at all, concerned ourselves with the examination of conflicting views and with argument about them. But before we end this chapter, we must examine three closely interconnected passages, the interpretation of which is very difficult. These passages are so difficult that we give the translation of each of them in five different versions. In each case we quote the translations in the following order—the Authorized Version, the Revised Version, the Revised Standard Version, the Moffatt translation, and the translation of The New Testament in Plain English, by C. Kingsley Williams.

The first passage is 1 Timothy 3[16], of which the translations are as follows:

> God was made manifest in the flesh
> Justified in the Spirit,
> Seen of angels,
> Preached unto the Gentiles.
> Believed on in the world,
> Received up into glory (AV).
>
> Justified in the spirit (RV).
>
> Vindicated in the Spirit (RSV).
>
> Vindicated by the Spirit (M.).
>
> Proved in the Spirit (C.K.W.).

The second passage is Romans 1[4], of which the translations are as follows:

Jesus Christ our Lord, which was made of the seed of David according to the flesh; and declared to be the Son of God with power, according to the spirit of holiness, by the resurrection from the dead (AV and RV).

> ... descended from David according to the flesh and designated Son of God in power according to the Spirit of holiness, by His resurrection from the dead, Jesus Christ our Lord (RSV).
>
> ... born of David's offspring by natural descent, and installed as Son of God with power by the Spirit of holiness when He was raised from the dead (M.).
>
> ... who as a man was born of David's line, and was appointed Son of God with power according to the Spirit of holiness, Jesus Christ our Lord by the resurrection from the dead (C.K.W.).

The third passage is 1 Peter 3[18] where it is said of Jesus:

> being put to death in the flesh, but quickened by the Spirit (AV).
>
> being put to death·in the flesh, but quickened in the spirit (RV).
>
> being put to death in the flesh but made alive in the spirit (RSV).
>
> in the flesh he was put to death but he came to life in the Spirit (M.).
>
> He was put to death in the flesh, but raised to life in the Spirit (C.K.W.).

The difficulty of these passages can be seen simply by setting down the different translations. One basic difference springs to the eye immediately. The translators who spell *Spirit* with a capital letter plainly take these passages as referring to the Holy Spirit; the translators who spell *spirit* with a small letter plainly take these passages as having nothing at all to do ,with the Holy Spirit, but as having to do with the spirit of Jesus, in the sense of which we speak of the spirit of a man, that is, the spiritual part of him as opposed to his physical body.

First, let us consider each of these passages on the assumption that the reference is to the *Holy Spirit*, and that the spelling with a capital letter is correct. The original Greek manuscripts are of no help here, for all the earliest and the best manuscripts, indeed all the manuscripts down until about the tenth century are uncial manuscripts. That is to say, they are written entirely in capital letters.

(*a*) 1 Timothy 3[16]. If we say that Jesus was vindicated, justified, or proved *by* the Spirit, it can mean one of two things. Either it means that the Holy Spirit is the assertor, as E. K. Simpson called Him, of the deity and lordship of Jesus Christ, witnessing in the hearts of men to the supremacy and godhead of Jesus, in spite of His death as a criminal upon a cross. Or it could mean that every one of Jesus' claims was vindicated by the coming of the Spirit upon the Church at the time of Pentecost. That event was a complete vindication of Him, because in it all His promises came true. Just possibly the phrase *justified in* or *by the Spirit* could mean that Jesus was made righteous, and kept sinless—as Walter Lock puts it, 'kept immaculate'—by the power of the Holy Spirit within Him, or that His claims were all vindicated and justified by the Spirit dwelling within Him, and thereby giving Him power to cast out devils, to conquer all evil, and finally to rise from the grave.

(*b*) Romans 1⁴. *According to the Spirit of holiness* could mean, Even as the Holy Spirit had foretold, that is, in the prophets. The whole passage would then mean that Jesus was born of the seed of David; He died; He was resurrected; by His resurrection He was fully designated Son of God; and all this happened as the Holy Spirit in the prophets had long since foretold. If the phrase be translated *By the Spirit of holiness*, then the only possible meaning is that the Holy Spirit was the agent of the Resurrection of Jesus Christ and of His exaltation into glory, the events which prove Him to be the Son of God.

(*c*) 1 Peter 3¹⁸. If we take this passage as referring to the Holy Spirit, we must also assume that *quickened by* or *in the Spirit* must mean that the Holy Spirit was God's effective agent in the Resurrection of Jesus Christ, that God, as it were, breathed life again into His Son by His Spirit.

If these passages do refer to the Holy Spirit, their quite extraordinary interest is that they all converge on the amazing conception that the Holy Spirit was God's agent in the Resurrection of Jesus Christ.

Second, let us consider these passages on the assumption that the reference is, not to the Holy Spirit, but to the spirit of Jesus, the spiritual part of Him, as contrasted with His physical body.

(*a*) 1 Timothy 3¹⁶. That could mean either of two things. It could mean that He was vindicated in His own conscience, as, indeed, we can see that He was by His words: 'Which of you convicteth me of sin?' (John 8⁴⁶). Or it could mean that.

once the Cross was over and once the body of His flesh was
laid aside, then came His Resurrection, and then, indeed, all
His claims were vindicated. That is to say, His vindication
came in His spiritual state.

(*b*) Romans 1⁴. If we say Jesus was declared to be the Son
of God *according to the spirit of holiness*, it can only mean that
Jesus was declared to be the Son of God, and Jesus was
resurrected from the dead, because of what Sanday and
Headlam describe as His 'exceptional and transcendent
holiness'. It was the holiness of the spirit, the life, the soul,
the mind, the inmost being of Jesus Christ, which distin-
guished Him from all men, which made Him sinless, and
which gave Him the right to be the Son of God, and which
made death powerless to hold Him.

(*c*) 1 Peter 3¹⁸. If we say that Jesus was put to death in the
flesh, and *quickened* or *made alive in the spirit*, it will mean, as
F. W. Beare puts it, that His death took place in the sphere of
the flesh, the earthly, temporal existence, and His resurrection
took place in the sphere of the spirit, the eternal, the indestructible, the heavenly. As Alford put it more fully, the meaning
will be: 'His flesh was the subject, recipient, vehicle of in-
flicted death; His spirit was the subject, recipient, vehicle of
restored life. . . . He the God-man Christ Jesus, body and soul,
ceased to live in the flesh, began to live in the spirit; ceased to
live a fleshly, mortal life, and began to live a spiritual, resurrection life.'

It is by no means easy to make up one's mind whereto the
reference of these passages is; but this much is certain—if
they are to be read as referring to the Holy Spirit at all, then
here we are shown the Holy Spirit's supreme and highest
function: He was God's agent in the Resurrection of God's
Son.

However that may be, and however uncertain may be the
interpretation of these three passages, it is abundantly clear
beyond all uncertainty that the Church of the New Testament
was the Church of the Holy Spirit.

CHAPTER SEVEN

The Holy Spirit and the Church Today

TODAY IN the middle of the twentieth century the Christian Church is confronted with challenge and with opportunity
in a way and on a scale that it has not known for centuries,
perhaps ever, before. This is a time of the emergence of
nations, with all the accompanying clash of race and of colour,
and all the problems of finding a new way of living together.
This is a time when humanity is genuinely faced with the
possibility of racial suicide, for men have acquired powers and
tapped forces with which they can quite easily destroy each
other and destroy themselves. This is a time of ecumenicity,
when the Church has become acutely conscious of the sin of
its divisions, and when it seems tragically unable to do anything to turn them into unity. It is true that this is a time
of religious indifference; but, strangely enough, it is also true
that this is a time of reawakened interest in religion. Even if
religion has to struggle against vast indifference, it is also true
that, even if it has not become a power and a force in the lives
of many, it has nevertheless become at least a talking-point
and a matter of argument and of discussion.

At such a time our thoughts inevitably go back to the days of
the early Church, days in which obviously the Church seethed
and surged with power. We must remember the beginning of
the story. When Jesus had been crucified and had risen again,
the sum total of the Church was one hundred and twenty
persons (Acts 1[15]). There was scarcely a man of wealth or
influence or power amongst them; there was scarcely a man of
intellectual eminence; they were poor, they were undis-
tinguished, and they were simple. To this little company of
people there was given an incredible task: 'Ye shall be witnesses unto me', said the Risen Christ, 'both in Jerusalem,

and in all Judaea, and in Samaria, and unto the uttermost part of the earth' (Acts 1[8]); 'Go ye and teach all nations' (Matthew 28[19]). The message which they were to bring was the story of a wandering Galilaean prophet, crucified as a criminal in Jerusalem. They were Jews, and they were to bring their message to a world where anti-Semitism was as violent as it has been at any time in history. They were to preach purity to a world which was steeped in immorality, and which for the most part did not even regard chastity as a virtue to be desired. On the face of it, it looked a task which was completely impossible. It would not have been in the least surprising from the human point of view, if those who were confronted with it had simply recognized its impossibility, and had not even begun to attempt it.

But before they began the task they were bidden to wait. To wait for what, or for whom? They were bidden to wait for the coming of the Holy Spirit upon them (Acts 1[4, 5, 8]). And when the Holy Spirit came, the task which seemed impossible somehow became possible. Within thirty years the message of the gospel had reached Rome and far beyond, the members of the Church were reckoned by the hundred thousand, and into the world there had come a new life and a new purity which not even those most hostile to Christianity could deny. The New Testament leaves us in not the slightest doubt that the power behind this miracle was the power of the Holy Spirit. It is that same power which the Church of today needs to confront the challenge and to grasp the opportunity. Let us, then, see certain areas and directions in which the Church cannot do without the things which only the Holy Spirit can bring.

Without the Holy Spirit the Church cannot have a *message*. It was through the Holy Spirit that the gospel was first preached, and it is through the Holy Spirit that the gospel must continue to be preached (1 Peter 1[12]). Preaching always inherently runs certain dangers. It may very easily become the airing of the preacher's own opinions and, worse, of his own prejudices. It may even become the expression of the preacher's own doubts and questionings. There has always been an attitude of mind which thinks that it is intellectually more respectable to be sceptical and agnostic than to be committed and certain. 'Tell me of your certainties', said Goethe; 'I have doubts enough of my own.' It may easily become trivial, skating round the circumference of the faith instead of clinging to the centre. In the few months before his tragically early death, Leslie Tizard remembered the words of J. B. Priestley, who said that people grew tired of 'having the front of their minds tickled' and wanted something deeper than that. It may easily grow irrelevant, spending time on answering questions which no one is asking, or discussing problems which are remote from the life of the hearers.

It is only the Holy Spirit who can save preaching from all these dangers. The man who has the experience of the Holy Spirit is the man who has a message, the man who can utter again the prophetic words: 'Thus saith the Lord.' The preacher may be a scholar, a pastor, an administrator, an ecclesiastical statesman, a scintillating orator, a social reformer. He is nothing unless he is a man of the Spirit.

Without the Holy Spirit the Church can have no accent of *certainty*. If ever men needed this accent of certainty, it is today. Max Warren, thinking particularly of areas like Africa where race and nationality are in the melting-pot, said a thing which is relevant anywhere today: 'Whether he [the teacher] is dealing with children or adults, he is dealing with people who are adrift from their moorings.' H. G. Wells expressed this vividly. He was thinking of the solidity and security of the Victorian age, and then of the following age in which two devastating wars removed all security, and in which there were social, economic, religious changes which amounted to a revolution. 'Queen Victoria', he said, 'was like a great paperweight, who had sat on men's minds for fifty years, and when she was removed their ideas began to blow about haphazardly all over the place.' Margaret Avery tells how a young person once said to her: 'The basic difference between your generation and mine is that we have never known what security means.' Beverley Nichols in *Are They the Same at Home* recorded interviews with several famous men. One was Hilaire Belloc, one of the greatest Roman Catholic laymen of his day. 'I was sorry for Mr Belloc', said Mr Nichols, 'because I knew that he had nailed at least some of his colours to the wrong mast, but I was sorrier still for myself and my own generation, because I knew that we had no colours of any kind to nail to any mast.' G. K. Chesterton once said that the difference between the modern generation and the generation which went before was that the older generation had seen things in terms of black and white, whereas the modern generation sees them in terms of an indeterminate grey.

One of the most famous novels of its generation was A. S. M. Hutchison's *If Winter Comes*, written away back in 1921. In it there is the picture of that tortured idealist, Mark Sabre. Mark's one desire is for light. He talks to his friend Hapgood: ' "Man cannot live by bread alone, the churches tell him; but he says, 'I *am* living on bread alone, and doing well on it.' But I tell you, Hapgood, that plumb down in the crypt and abyss of every man's soul is a hunger, a craving for other food than this earthly stuff. And the Churches know it; and instead of reaching down to him what he wants—light, light—instead of that, they invite him to dancing and picture-shows, and you're a jolly good fellow, and religion's a jolly fine thing and no spoil-sport, and all that sort of latter-day tendency. Why, man, he can get all that outside the churches and get it better. Light, light! He wants light, Hapgood. And the padres come down and drink beer with him, and watch boxing-matches with him, and dance Jazz with him, and call it making religion a Living Thing in the Lives of the People. Lift the hearts of the people to God, they say, by showing them that religion is not incompatible with having a jolly fine time. *And there's no God there that a man can understand for him to be lifted to.* Hapgood, a man wouldn't care *what* he had to give up if he knew he was making for something inestimably precious. But he doesn't know. Light, Light—that's what he wants; and the longer it's withheld the lower he'll sink. Light! Light!" '

That is an amazing passage to find in a novel, and these are words which, to us who are within the Church, are intensely challenging. This is not a condemnation of social fellowship within the Church; but it is the reminder that social fellowship within the Church exists to produce the human relationship between man and man and preacher and people in which the higher things can be approached together, and God sought and found together. It is never an end in itself; it is always a means towards creating a situation in which people know each other so well that they seek God together.

G. K. Chesterton once said that we have asked all the questions which can be asked, and that it is time we stopped asking the questions, and started looking for the answers. There is no way to this essential certainty other than through the Holy Spirit. We can only stop saying: 'I think that it may be so,' and begin saying, 'I know that it is so,' through the help of the Holy Spirit. Study, discussion, argument are all good and all necessary, but all futile unless the Holy Spirit be there to reveal and to communicate that certainty for which modern man craves. No Church can dare to face the needs of a generation adrift from its moorings without the help of the Holy Spirit.

Without the Holy Spirit, and without an intense belief in the Holy Spirit, no Church can have any real *growth and development* in its faith and in its belief. The tragedy of orthodoxy is that it is so often conceived of in static terms; it is conceived of as something which does not and which cannot change, even in expression; and any change becomes heresy.

Collie Knox told in an article of what happened to him during the last national census. He got into trouble with the collector of the census papers because there was one column in which he refused to insert an answer. The question at the head of the column which was the cause of dispute was: 'At what age did you finish your education?' Collie Knox insisted that he had never finished it, and that he was being educated yet! The danger which any Church runs is the danger of what

Harnack described as 'worshipping its own past'. It seems extraordinary that anyone should seriously believe that Christianity can still be presented to people in categories of thought and forms of expression which are well on for two thousand years old. This problem is not so acute for people inside the Church, for they have been for long, many of them from childhood, familiar with the words and the ideas which are used. But for those outside the Church the barrier is well-nigh insurmountable.

This is a problem which only a vivid awareness of the Holy Spirit can solve. Without the Holy Spirit even the Bible becomes a dead letter, and the credal statements of the Church becomes fossilized antiquities. J. H. Oldham once said: 'We must dare in order to know.' It is entirely necessary that we should entrust ourselves to the guidance of the Holy Spirit in order that we may rethink and restate the message of the gospel for the generation in which we live. Only when faith and belief depend, not on a book and not on a creed, but on the living Spirit of the living God, can the faith and belief of the Church grow and develop in such a way that both the Church's belief and the statement of it are never out of date.

Without the Holy Spirit there can be no real *fellowship* within the Church. Sunday after Sunday we pray for the fellowship of the Holy Spirit, the fellowship which the Spirit can bring and give and maintain. Division is the characteristic of natural man; unity is the characteristic of Christian man. 'By this shall all men know that ye are my disciples, if ye have love one to another' (John 13[35]). As John bluntly puts it in his letter: 'If any man say, I love God, and hateth his brother, he is a liar' (1 John 4[20]).

W. H. Davies, the tramp poet, has a very interesting and significant picture in one of his volumes of autobiography. He tells how he was in Ebbw Vale in Wales. He saw two men who were slightly drunk. Another man passed. One of the men said to the other: 'Is that an Abertillery man?' And, as he said it, his face was angry and his fists were clenched. 'No,' replied the other man. Now, says, Davies, if that man had been an Abertillery man, these two Ebbw Vale men would have set upon him without provocation, and would have beaten him up. Why? Because there is a steep, rough mountain between Ebbw Vale and Abertillery, and the mountain prevented the two towns from growing and joining together, and for that reason their people were bitter enemies. I cannot tell whether that situation still exists, but one may well call it 'the sin of mountains'. It is human nature to be suspicious, hostile, towards the stranger.

The curious and the distressing feature about Churches is the amount of bickering and difference and dispute and often long-lasting bitterness which arises within them about matters of personal prestige, and rights, and place, and position and the like. Nothing could better prove the absence of the Holy Spirit.

We speak much in these days about ecumenicity, and yet we do heart-breakingly little to achieve it in any real sense of the term. This will continue to be so, so long as the different branches of the Church put systems and forms, histories and traditions, rights and privileges, before the presence of the Holy Spirit. It is a literally shocking thing even to imply that the Holy Spirit can operate within only one form of Church government or Church belief.

Max Warren quotes a definition, by W. C. Willoughby, in *The Christian Imperative*, in which fellowship is described as 'the joy of going through life hand in hand with the comrade of one's choice, sharing one another's burdens, stimulating one another's courage, doubling one another's sagacity, buckling on one another's armour, wearing one another's laurels, and easing one another's pain'. That is a situation impossible without the Holy Spirit.

It is only when men and Churches walk together in the atmosphere of the Spirit that true fellowship can come. There is little use in praying for the fellowship of the Holy Spirit and then shutting the Spirit out.

Without the Holy Spirit there can be no adequate doctrine or experience of *conversion*. It is one of the significant features

of the present time that the word and the experience of conversion have been rediscovered in the orthodox Church. With
that rediscovery there has come a very real danger, the kind of
danger which comes from the confusion of half the truth with
the whole truth. The danger is that the experience of conversion may come to be looked upon as the end of the road,
and that the person who has undergone the experience of
conversion may regard himself as a complete and perfected
Christian. The ordinary methods of mass evangelism have
inevitably increased that danger. The invitation so often is to
decide for Jesus Christ, and thereupon to find rest and peace
and joy. But there is more to it than that. It is perfectly true
that in the moment of conversion a new relationship is discovered between God and man, and in that discovery there is
a piercing and a radiant joy. But it is also true that, once a
man has decided for Jesus Christ, then his troubles begin.
Did not Jesus Himself warn men that following Him involved
daily saying No to oneself, and daily taking up a cross? Once
a man decides for Jesus Christ a new set of standards and
values enter into his life. Things which he once accepted with
equanimity he must now regard with horror. A goodness and
a purity which he never regarded as relevant for him become
obligatory on him. A new sensitiveness to, and awareness of,
sin enter into his life. A new responsibility accompanies the
new privilege of which he has become aware. And unless he
realizes that there is such a person as the Holy Spirit, unless he
lays hold upon the power of the Holy Spirit, unless the Holy
Spirit daily lives more in him and he in the Holy Spirit, then
the experience of conversion will necessarily lead to nowhere
but disappointment, disillusionment and frustration. That is
why so many of those who experience the conversions which
accompany mass evangelism never last the course, but relapse
into their old way of life.

Conversion cannot stop at confronting a man with the Cross,
even if it must begin there. It must go on to tell a man of the
Risen Christ, of the power of the Spirit, of the new life which
the Spirit makes possible. The moment of conversion or of

decision must be followed by the life of the Spirit. To put it in Pauline language, justification is irrelevant unless it is followed by sanctification. It ought to be the determination of every evangelist to preach the Holy Spirit as much as he preaches the Cross. Christ died for men is a glorious truth; but Christ lives for men in the Holy Spirit is an equally glorious truth.

Without the Holy Spirit there can be no true *worship* in the Church. The fact about the worship of the Church which sometimes drives a man to a kind of wondering despair is that nothing seems to happen. It may have beauty, it may sometimes have a hot wind of emotion, but it so seldom has *power*. A. J. Gossip used to tell how Thomas Chalmers was once congratulated on a masterpiece of a speech delivered in the General Assembly of the Church of Scotland. 'Yes', said Chalmers, 'but what *happened*?' There lies the test. Aesthetic enjoyment of beauty, exhilarating experience of emotion, are no substitute for power.

In *When We Two Walked* Rita Snowden tells of a walking-tour she and a friend made in the south of England. On a Sunday they came to a little village church, and they went in. There were three in the choir, perhaps twenty in the congregation, and the Vicar. 'Hymn and psalm and prayer, and the quiet murmuring voice of the Vicar tended to take my thoughts out of the windows into the morning sunlight and over the fields and far away. The pity is, it was all so harmless, so gentle, so proper.' There was nothing to remind anyone of 'that Young Man who strode the countryside and talked with the country people of Galilee, in burning words. . . . The kind of Man who leaves you restless ever afterwards until you have found His God, and learned to call Him "Father" too.' That is a recognizable picture, the kind of worship in which there is a drowsy peace which is much more likely to send a man to sleep than to compel him to participate with loins girt and with lamp burning. And even when worship is hearty and intense and momentarily rousing, there is so often the same ineffectiveness.

True worship must be worship in the Spirit. In that kind of worship the people participate as much as the preacher. That kind of worship will never be found where either preacher or people is unprepared. The true worship in the Spirit cannot be found in a company of people who come to Church with as little preparation of their own spirits as they would go to a concert. If the people came to Church in preparation and in expectation, if the preacher committed himself and his message to the Spirit of God, then, and not till then, the flood tides of power would be unloosed upon men.

Let us take the matter to an even wider sphere than that. Without the Holy Spirit there can be no *unification* of life. The great mistake into which most of us more or less fall is the division of life into sacred and secular, into one part which belongs directly to God and one part which is more or less our business, into one part in which we are aware of the presence of God and one part where we almost forget that God exists. But life in the Spirit would necessarily mean that there is no part of life which is not sacred. No man can get out of the air in which he breathes, and no Christian ought to be able to get out of the Holy Spirit.

The truly great Christians well knew this. David Livingstone once wrote: 'I am serving Christ when shooting a buffalo for my men, or taking an astronomical observation, or writing to one of His children who forget.' Max Warren tells of a letter from an African headmaster to a friend of his who had given a course of talks in that African school. The letter ran: 'We appreciated your helpful talks on the application of the teaching of Jesus Christ in our agricultural work and hygiene, as well as in spiritual things. Until now we regarded agriculture and hygiene as merely secular subjects, without any connection with Christianity.'

It was Brother Lawrence who said that he felt as near to God when he was washing the dirty dishes in the monastery kitchen as he did at the blessed Sacrament. Kipling's engineer McAndrew saw God in the engines of his ship:

From coupler-flange to spindle-guide I see Thy Hand, O God—
Predestination in the stride o' yon connectin'-rod.

Unless a man lives in the Holy Spirit, he can never experience this unification of life, this all-embracing presence of God, this world in which he is always aware that in God he lives and moves and has his being.

In one last sphere the Holy Spirit is a necessity. Without the Holy Spirit it is not possible for a man fully *to cope with life*. Certainly a man may *exist* without the Holy Spirit, but equally certainly he cannot *live* without the Holy Spirit. There are three gifts which all men need, and which the Holy Spirit can give.

In the days in which we live we need *courage*. There was literally never a time in history when the future was so frightening. There have been times when men have been faced with the break-up of the nation of which they were a part; there have been times when the tides of barbarism threatened to sweep over the world; there have been times when men were threatened with economic ruin; there have been times when men were threatened with slavery and suffering and death. But never before was there a time when men were threatened with the end of humanity and the disintegration of the universe by their own actions. Even before men had tapped the secrets of atomic power, C. M. Joad once said that the trouble with the world was that men had the powers of gods and used them like irresponsible schoolboys. In the days between the wars, when the first World War was still remembered, and when the second World War was already a menacing shadow on the horizon, Sir Philip Gibbs wrote: 'If I smell poison gas in Edgware Road, I am not going to put on a gas-mask, or go to a gas-proof room. I am going out to take a good sniff of it; for I shall know that the game is up.' *The game is up*—that is precisely the feeling which is in the hearts of men today. There is a strange parallel between this age and the days of the Roman Empire in the first Christian century, just at the very time when Christianity was being preached, when the New Testament was being written, and when Paul was in Rome. In those days there were thinking men who felt that life was too dangerous to contemplate, that honour was too precious to lose, that civilization was too rotten to continue, and they therefore extolled the virtues of suicide. This is specially true of the Stoics. 'God', they said, 'gave men life, and He gave them the even greater gift of being able to take their own lives away.' Seneca hears God say: 'Above all I have provided that none may hold you against your will; the door is open; nothing I have made more easy than to die; and death is quick.'

In such a situation Tillich is right when he says that what men need is not security but courage. That courage cannot be obtained from a man's inner resources. Even if we were to remove from life all the threats which are characteristics of the twentieth century, and leave only the perils, the threats, the dangers which are inherent in the chances and the changes of this earthly and this mortal life, that would still be true. H. G. Wells tells in his Autobiography of an experience of his own. It was in New York Harbour. His ship was nosing its way out in a fog, and in the fog it missed collision with another ship by a matter of yards. He goes on: 'The two boats had sucked in toward each other as they passed. Some of us tried to imagine just what a touch would have meant. Nobody was very much upset about it; it seemed just a part of the general large dangerousness of human affairs at the present time.' Life is essentially dangerous. And, further, no creature is so vulnerable as man, vulnerable not only to pain and death, but, what is far worse, vulnerable to sorrow and to all the wounds which cause the imperious anguish of the heart.

Here is the human situation. In our own strength it may be borne, but it cannot be conquered. If we are to face this life in victorious living, we cannot do so otherwise than in the strength of the Holy Spirit of God, in the awareness that God is with us.

In any time in life we need *guidance*. 'Life', as it has been said, 'concentrates upon man at the cross-roads.' There is no map of life, for a very simple reason: there are no fixed roads in life. If we wish to make a geographical journey from Glasgow to London, there are fixed roads, and there are organizations which will provide us with an itinerary in which the wayfaring man, even if he be a fool, cannot err. But in the spiritual journey from, say, eighteen years of age to fifty years of age there is no itinerary. Every man has to hack out his own way, and make his own map, and take his own route. Therefore we need guidance, not advice from other men who know only their own road, but guidance from some mind and authority and wisdom which stands outside life and sees all life. That guidance can only come to us from the Holy Spirit, from God acting and speaking in our lives, from Jesus Christ still with us in the Spirit whom He promised to us.

In any time in life we need *power*. Our difficulty is seldom to know what to do; our difficulty is to do it. It is not lack of knowledge of goodness which troubles us; it is the inability to be good. It was Archimedes who discovered the principle of the lever, that if you place a lever below a mass, you can lift the mass, and the longer the lever the heavier the mass you can lift. Archimedes said: 'Give me a lever long enough, and give me a place outside the world to stand, and I will lift the world.' It was from *outside* the world had to be lifted. Even so with us. So long as we are dependent only on ourselves, the result of all effort can only be frustration. It is only in the power of the Spirit, bringing to us the strength of God and the grace of Jesus Christ, that we can attain to the goodness, to which we ought to attain, and to which we fail to attain.

> *And every virtue we possess,*
> *And every victory won,*
> *And every thought of holiness,*
> *Are His alone.*

When we have said all this, it is inevitable that one question should rise from our hearts and be on our lips—How can we receive this Spirit? Love, joy, peace, long-suffering, gentleness, goodness, fidelity, meekness, self-control—these are the fruit of the Spirit (Galatians 5$^{22-3}$). How is this fruit to appear in our lives?

The answer is an answer which our generation finds it hard to accept. W. B. Yeats says in his autobiography: 'Can one reach God by toil? He gives Himself to the pure in heart. He asks nothing but attention.' *He asks nothing but attention.* The only way to receive the Spirit is silently and prayerfully to wait upon the Spirit. We live in an age which has a pathetic faith in administration, efficiency, new and better methods, more and more effort, a faster and faster tempo. But the truth is that there can never be efficient activity without wise passivity at the back of it. Lionel Johnson, scholar and poet, once said to Yeats: 'Yeats, you need ten years in a library, but I need ten years in the wilderness.' For an age which believes in incessant action, silent waiting is an unpalatable prescription. For a man whose every waking moment is occupied, and who even steals time for work from the hours of sleep, there may be necessary a complete reorganization of life if he is to find time for this silent waiting on the Spirit. In a Church life in which the Church is increasingly highly organised, and in which strenuous activity is the key-note, and in which action is valued above all things, it is hard to find time for that apparent doing nothing which means everything. We may well remember the prophet's symbolic story of the man who was given a prisoner to guard and who allowed him to escape, and who, when he was called to account, gave as his excuse: 'As thy servant was busy here and there, he was gone' (1 Kings 20^{40}). It may well be that we are so busy here and there that the greatest of all powers is gone from our lives. 'They that wait upon the Lord', says Isaiah, 'shall renew their strength; they shall mount up with wings as eagles; they shall run, and not be weary; they shall walk, and not faint' (Isaiah 40^{31}). Without the waiting the power will never come.

In his book, *Living in Depth*, Dr James Reid has a sermon on Pentecost. He concludes it with these words: 'A Negro Salvationist was found one day kneeling in front of a tablet in a church commemorating the conversion there of General

Booth. "O Lord, do it again," he was praying over and over again. As we read the story of Pentecost and think of the world today and of the impotence of the Church, the same prayer will come to our lips, "O Lord, do it again".' Both for us and for the Church God will do it again, if we remember that He asks nothing but our attention, and if we learn to wait intensely on Him.

Index of Scripture Passages